THE EGO AND THE BIBLE

Stories of Divinely Intended Ego

Author: Greg Little

Copyright © 2014 Greg Little
All rights reserved.

ISBN: 1500759155
ISBN 13: 9781500759155
Library of Congress Control Number: 2014914137
CreateSpace Independent Publishing Platform
North Charleston, South Carolina

Contents

Foreword vii
Introduction xi
Chapter 1 In the Beginning: The Creation of Ego 1
Chapter 2 Cain and Abel: Brothers in Arms. 8
Chapter 3 Abraham: The Called 12
Chapter 4 Jacob the Trickster 21
Chapter 5 Joseph the Dreamer. 32
Chapter 6 Moses the Law Giver 41
Chapter 7 Samson the Blind Hero 50
Chapter 8 Saul: King and Prophet. 55
Chapter 9 David: King and Visionary 59
Chapter 10 Solomon the Wise. 66
Chapter 11 Esther the Queen 71
Chapter 12 The Trials of Job. 78
Chapter 13 Jonah: Encountering God in the Belly of the Beast. 85
Chapter 14 Jeremiah: Receiver of the Word. 90
Chapter 15 Huldah the Prophetess 95
Chapter 16 Daniel: Tamer of Lions and Interpreter of Dreams 98
Chapter 17 Jesus of Nazareth: Christ and Messiah 109
Chapter 18 Mary: The God Bearer 124
Chapter 19 Satan: The Tempter. 131
Chapter 20 Jesus: From Wilderness to the Cross 137
Chapter 21 Judas: Betrayer or Servant 146
Chapter 22 Jesus: From Last Supper to Triumph 150

Chapter 23 Paul: Founder of Christianity 160
        Conclusion 169
        About the Author 171
        Bibliography 173

Figures and Credits

Figure 1   Expulsion from the Garden of Eden, Tommaso Cassai Masaccio

Figure 2   Cain-murdering Able, Bartolomeo Manfredi circa-1610

Figure 3   Abraham, Sarah and Hagar, imagined here in a Bible illustration from 1897.

Figure 4   Jacob's Ladder, William Blake

Figure 5   Joseph and Potiphar's Wife, Joseph leaving, Orazio Gentileschi

Figure 6   Pharaoh's Daughter Finds Baby Moses, Nicolas Poussin_ 1638

Figure 7   The Blinded Samson, Franz Heinrich Louis Corinth, 1912

Figure 8   Saul-and the witch of Endor, Benjamin West 1777

Figure 9   David Giving Thanks to God After the Death of Goliath, 18th century painting attributed to Charles Errard the Young

Figure 10   Solomon and The Queen of Sheba, De Min, Giovanni (1789–1859),

Figure 11   Queen Esther (1878) as imagined by Edwin Long

Figure 12	The Examination of Job, Satan pours on the plagues of Job, by William Blake
Figure 13	Joseph and Potiphar's Wife, Joseph leaving by Orazio Gentileschi
Figure 13	Jonah Cast Forth By The Whale, Gustave Doré
Figure 14	The Prophet Jeremiah by Michelangelo
Figure 15	Daniel's Answer to the King by Briton Rivière
Figure 16	Adoration of the Magi by Fra Angelico and Filippo Lippi
Figure 17	The Temptation of Christ sixteenth-century master illuminator Simon Bening
Figure 18	Annunciation, Paolo de Matteis, 1712
Figure 19	Statue of the Fallen Angel, Retiro Park (Madrid, Spain,) Luis García (Zaqarbal)
Figure 20	Jesus enters Jerusalem and the crowds welcome him, Pietro Lorenzetti, 1320
Figure 21	Kiss of Judas (1304–06), fresco by Giotto, Scrovegni Chapel, Padua, Italy
Figure 22	The Mocking of Chris, Cavalier d'Arpino
Figure 23	The Conversion on the Way to Damascus, Caravaggio

Foreword

The subtitle of this book is adapted from the phrase "Divinely Intended Tension," coined by Friedrich von Hügel. This phrase has resonated with me from the moment I read it. The source of this revelation was a paragraph in a book by Paul Clasper:

> The mixture of ordinary, universal life was accepted as "normal" until the new life appeared which makes all previous life look old by comparison. In fact, one of the most startling features of the new life of the Way is the emerging of a vivid sense of new tension which had not existed before. The new produces a dynamic tension within the old life. Baron Friedrich von Hügel, the inspired lay Roman Catholic spiritual director of the last generation, used to call this the Divinely Intended Tension.[1]

I understand the term to mean the creative tension between opposites, which Carl Jung calls the transcendent third, to enter into a person's psyche. This transcendent third is the force that enables an individual to mature and grow to bring about the transformation progress along the path that Carl Jung named individuation. In turn, this will lead the Ego to function in service of the divine. Jung has named the archetype of the divine in the psyche the Self. In the absence of the individuation process, the Ego will rule actions of the individual, who may or may not

---

[1] Paul Clasper, *Eastern Paths and the Christian Way*, 85.

be conscious of this, and this individual's basic position in life will be egocentric.

In plain language, the Ego is what makes me, me. It is my awareness of myself as an individual separate and apart from the rest of the world. If our Egos are a gift from God—indeed one of the greatest of gifts—what does it mean for humankind to have Egos today? Our Egos make us who we are in this world. They enable us to live and survive and thrive in the world. If it were not for our Egos, we would not be conscious of who we are, or how we relate to the world around us. Our Egos give us the energy and drive to form and transform the world around us.

The following is a poem I composed that speaks to my experience of Divinely Intended Tension.

Divinely Intended Tension

Between what was
> And what will be.

Between the Being
> And the Becoming

I wait suspended
> In the awful Now.

That is neither
> And both

The Divinely Intended Tension
> Holds me firmly
> In its grasp

FOREWORD

Suspended over
>   The witch's cauldron
That wrathful brew
>   Waiting for me
To Succumb to the
>   Fumes of fear
That threatens to consume me.

And yet I cannot go back
To that place of pseudo harmony
>   And lost innocence
So all that remains
>   Is to remain.
In the hope that all
>   This is part
Of some great plan
Designed for God only knows
>   What purpose?

Introduction

> Then God said, "Let us make humankind in our image, according to our likeness; and let them have dominion over the fish of the sea, and over the birds of the air, and over the cattle, and over all the wild animals of the earth, and over every creeping thing that creeps upon the earth."[2]

Consciousness and its manifestation, Ego, separate human beings from the rest of God's creations. Indeed, it can be argued that when God set out to create humankind in God's image, consciousness and its complement, Ego, were the aspects that make human beings in the image of God.

For an understanding of what I mean by Ego, let us turn to C. G. Jung, one of the founders of modern depth psychology. Jung says, "By the Ego I understand a complex representation which constitutes the centre of my field of consciousness and appears to possess a very high degree of continuity and identity."[3]

The Ego is a direct outcome of consciousness. "For Jung, the Ego arose gradually out of unconsciousness—both in the infant and the species and returns to it every night...The Ego separates us from nature and replaces instinctive deciding, valuing, etc. It's a differentiated aspect of

---

[2] Genesis 1:26.
[3] Jolande Székács Jacobi, *The Psychology of Jung: An Introduction with Illustrations*, Google Books, 6.

the collective unconscious (compare Freud's Ego, derived from id). The Ego, then, is a kind of projection or fiction devised by the unconscious. Without an ego, a perceiving subject, nothing is perceived."[4]

As with many aspects of human psychology, Ego can be a gift or a curse, depending on how it is perceived and used. In Jungian terms, the material from the unconscious will have both a positive and a negative aspect. This is certainly true of the Ego. Egos are absolutely necessary for us to get on in life. We exist in relation to the world around us and in relation to others. We form families and other close relationships, work at jobs, live in neighbourhoods, accumulate material possessions, and seek to fill our lives with meaningful things. All these actions stem from and require the Ego.

Jung notes that consciousness does not lead to self-awareness:

> Anyone who has any ego-consciousness at all takes it for granted that he knows himself. But the Ego knows only its own contents, not the unconscious and its contents. People measure their self-knowledge by what the average person in their social environment knows of himself, but not by the real psychic facts which are for the most part hidden from them. In this respect the psyche behaves like the body, of whose physiological and anatomical structure the average person knows very little too.[5]

---

4 Cited at http://www.terrapsych.com/jungdefs.html
5 *The Undiscovered Self*, CW 10, par. 491.

INTRODUCTION

However, as it enables us to do so much, Ego also creates a level of desire that is often not beneficial to us, to others, or to the world. One good example of this refers to the "driven ego," in which the Ego encompasses "enslavement to gratification and obsessive self-centeredness."[6] Consider that the Ego, as a part of the psyche, has autonomy. As an autonomous force, it believes, at a fundamental level, that it is the centre of everything important, and it acts accordingly. The Ego has everything invested in the status quo. Because its job is to protect the psyche of the person, the Ego does not want any change. Richard Rohr has noted that Ego first occurs when we split from the world, early in our existence in this world:

> The first split is very understandable. We split ourselves from other selves. We see our mommy and our daddy, and they're over there, and we're over here. I start looking out at life with myself as the center point. It's the beginning of egocentricity. My ego is the center; what I like, what I want, what I need is what matters. And I'm going to let Mama know what I want! It is so nice to have a personal slave for a few years, but some never get over it.[7]

It may seem counterintuitive that the Ego has, in effect, a mind of its own and is autonomous from our will. However, this was recognized in ancient times as indicated by St. Paul, "I do not understand my own actions. For I do not do what I want, but I do the very thing I hate."[8] Jung noted that the energy that is contained in the unconscious is

---
6 *Different Directions to our Divinity; A Centre for Conscious Care.*
7 Richard Rohr, Daily Meditations, *Splitting from Others,* Tuesday, February 25, 2014.
8 Romans 7:15. All biblical quotes are from the NRSV unless otherwise indicated.

THE EGO AND THE BIBLE

autonomous. In effect it operates under what seems to be a central will that is separate from our conscious life. The Ego has its origin in the unconscious being. As noted by Paul Levy, it is "a kind of projection or fiction devised by the unconscious. Without an ego, a perceiving subject, nothing is perceived."[9] As such it operates autonomously from our conscious will.

Unless checked, the Ego will attempt to achieve security for a person by any means available it believes necessary to achieve the resulting happiness. Unless the Ego is reined in by a greater force—physical, moral, or spiritual—it will stop at almost nothing to achieve its ends. As such, the Ego can be a gift, or it can be a curse.

If the Ego is truly a gift of God, as I believe, it stands to reason that we are intended to use that divine gift for God's purpose. In that case, the role of the Ego has played an important part in the story of God's interaction with his work of creation on the sixth day. I intend, therefore, to examine the part that the Ego has played in the record of God's people—the Christian Bible. In the following pages, I will examine some of the stories of the people of God, along with how their Egos factored into those stories—for better and for worse.

---

9 http://www.awakeninthedream.com/wordpress/glossary-of-terms/#complexes

Chapter 1

In the Beginning: The Creation of Ego

> Then the Lord God said, "See, the man has become like one of us, knowing good and evil; and now, he might reach out his hand and take also from the tree of life, and eat, and live for ever"—therefore the Lord God sent him forth from the garden of Eden, to till the ground from which he was taken. He drove out the man; and at the east of the Garden of Eden he placed the cherubim, and a sword flaming and turning to guard the way to the tree of life.[10]

In the creation myth (I use this term in the sense of story that carries eternal truth), God declares his judgement on the first parents, the progenitors of the human race. Adam and Eve are given something that set them apart in creation: they become godlike, knowing good and evil. This judgement of God is, contrary to Christian doctrine, not truly a judgement at all. The expulsion is a consequence of a gift from that same creator of the gift itself, the gift of *gnosis*—knowledge of good and evil—means that they could no longer reside in the garden in a state of pure innocence, walking in the cool of the evening with their

---

10   Genesis 3:22–24.

creator. They now possess something that would be a blessing and a curse—consciousness that they are separate from the rest of creation, separate from each other, and, most of all, separate from their creator. Adam and Eve now possess Egos. Let us look at this gift of the Ego from God. How did it come about, and how did it manifest itself when it was received? Adam and Eve were created in God's image on the sixth day. In creating them, God declares the Ego good; indeed, God declares it very good. What then makes humankind in God's image? We are not told in the narrative what characteristics fulfilled these criteria. Does this mean that humans are formed in the physical image of God? I understand it would be childish to believe that God is in the physical form of humans or vice versa—or that God is a great being in the sky or elsewhere. What "in the image of God" refers to, at least in part, is the gift of consciousness. Our consciousness sets humans apart from the rest of creation and makes us a reflection of the image of God. We are, therefore, creatures who know we are separate from our creator, and we must deal with that knowledge.

IN THE BEGINNING: THE CREATION OF EGO

Figure 1 Expulsion from the Garden of Eden

Jung speaks to this gift of God which resulted in the expulsion of humankind from the Garden of Eden: "There is deep doctrine in the legend on the Fall; it is the expression of dim presentiment that the emancipation of ego-consciousness was a Luciferian deed."[11]

---

11 *Mysterium Coniunctionis,* CW 14, pars. 544ff.

THE EGO AND THE BIBLE

We humans gained the knowledge as a gift from God, though it did not seem like a gift in its giving. God set the first human creatures in the garden to live in a natural state of complete innocence before their eyes were opened, before they knew they were naked. This natural state of innocence was shattered by the serpent that tempted them—or rather tempted Eve—to eat of the fruit of the tree, which had been denied them by their God. Upon being tempted, Eve ate of the fruit of the knowledge of good and evil and then gave the fruit to Adam, and their eyes were opened. So, how is this knowledge a gift—if they possessed it in opposition to the direct command by God? A question also arises of why God placed this tree within such apparent, easy reach of his greatest creation if He did not intend them to eat it. Why did God place the serpent—another of his creations—in the garden to tempt them if He had no intention that they would taste of that divine fruit that would give them the gift of knowledge—when it was this gift that would separate them from the rest of creation and from God Himself? He could only have done this if He intended for them to taste of this greatest gift—consciousness—and begin the creation of Ego which would lead to the first parents and all humans becoming aware that they were separate from God and the rest of creation. Jung addresses this Luciferian gift in a positive take on the role of the serpent:

> Man's whole history consists from the very beginning in a conflict between his feelings of inferiority and his arrogance. Wisdom seeks the middle path and pays for this audacity by a dubious affinity with daemon and beast, and so is open to moral interpretation.[12]

---
12 *The Archetype and the Collective Unconscious*, 230.

IN THE BEGINNING: THE CREATION OF EGO

This gift was given in the manner it was out of necessity, as its very nature necessitates its ambiguity—it is a gift and a blessing. It must be stolen from God if it is to give what it is intended to give. For humankind to know we are unique and separate from the rest of creation, we must separate ourselves from God in an act of childlike rebellion and disobedience. The act of divine disobedience in the Garden of Eden sets humankind free from the natural state of bliss in which we experienced union with God as well as nature. Our eyes were opened, and we knew we were naked; we knew shame for the first time.

What, then, is the result of this knowledge? Well, as we know, the first thing that was done was to avoid responsibility. Adam blamed his gnosis on Eve: "The woman who you gave me, she gave me the fruit from the tree, and I ate." Notice the first awakening of the subtlety with which Adam now justifies himself. Not only does he deflect the blame from himself, but he implies that God is also to blame for giving him a partner who would do such a thing. Eve is not to be outdone. She just as easily blames the serpent: "The serpent tricked me, and I ate." How natural and easy these prevarications come to these newly conscious creatures. It is a precursor of things to come.

The ambiguity of the newly formed Ego is revealed in how these events have been viewed in the millennia that followed. This blessing and curse of God has never been seen for what it is. After all, it led to our expulsion from the garden where there was no sorrow and no sweat of the brow and no anxiety. Now we work for our existence, "Now in toil you shall eat of it all the days of your life." "Women will in pain give birth." "We are dust and to dust we shall return." No wonder our current state was condemned by the descendants of the first parents. We also needed someone to blame for our separateness from the creator. The creation myth is also understood as an explanation for our mortality. Why is it that we are "dust and to dust we shall return," as God's judgement proclaims? This phrase is not a punishment, but rather it is a consequence of our consciousness. Unlike the rest of creation, we are aware of our mortality and will have to face that reality. Our Egos will try to deny this fact, but we eventually have to face this mortality. Edward Edinger speaks to the expulsion from Paradise as being grounded in the material world, drawing on the alchemical tradition:

> Eating the fruit in the Garden of Eden belongs to coagulatio symbolism and represents a "grounding" process accompanying conscious realization. Hence the text just quoted states that Adam is cast "out of Paradise down upon the earth," implying that heretofore he had not quite been born into earthly existence.[13]

The consciousness with which humankind has been endowed by God, as I've noted, led to humans having Egos. Before continuing, let me further clarify what I mean by Ego. I am using the definition as the conscious self; the "I." The Ego is the central, experience-filtering complex of consciousness and is the most stable complex because it's grounded in the bodily sensations.[14] In contrast to the Ego, the Self is the central complex of the collective unconscious. The Self is a concept originated by Jung, which he postulated contains all the energies of the unconscious such as archetypes and complexes. When it is contained in dreams it

---

13 *The Bible and the Psyche*, 20.
14 http://www.terrapsych.com/jungdefs.html

IN THE BEGINNING: THE CREATION OF EGO

will present an image of wholeness to the conscious mind in forms such as mandalas and other circles. The impact of this self-awareness, which began in our Eden home and led to our expulsion from paradise, did not end there. The impact of the Ego on humankind in our relations with each other and with God has had what I would consider to be a formative effect from the first day outside the walls of that primordial home. This impact is described in the events recorded in the Holy Scripture, which contains that creation story. In the following pages I will explore how the Ego influences some of the stories contained in the Christian Bible.

Chapter 2

Cain and Abel: Brothers in Arms

> Cain said to his brother Abel, "Let us go out to the field." And when they were in the field, Cain rose up against his brother Abel and killed him. Then the LORD said to Cain, "Where is your brother Abel?" He said, "I do not know; am I my brother's keeper?"[15]

Thus the story of the first murder is also the first case of fratricide. Cain rises up in anger and strikes down his brother, Abel. However, let us look at the case of Cain's anger.

Cain is a tiller of the field, whereas Abel is a keeper of sheep. Both brothers offer the first fruits of their particular produce to God. God accepts Abel's offering, but "for Cain and his offering He had no regard." Cain is angry with God, who rebuked him:

> The LORD said to Cain, "Why are you angry, and why has your countenance fallen? If you do well, will you not be accepted? And if you do not do well, sin is lurking at the door; its desire is for you, but you must master it."[16]

---

15 Genesis 4:8-9.
16 Genesis 4:6-7.

CAIN AND ABEL: BROTHERS IN ARMS

However, God does not explain, to Cain or to us, why Cain's offering is not accepted. Cain knows he could not take his anger out on the all-powerful creator, so he deflects it onto the one whose offering is acceptable—Abel. Cain would be jealous of his brother, making Abel an easy target for his anger. Cain's disappointment at having his own offering rejected by the Most High God, and having no explanation and therefore no way of knowing how to make his offering worthy, leads to the first murder and launches humankind on a path that would produce many mountains of corpses.

Figure 2 Cain Murdering Abel, circa 1610

THE EGO AND THE BIBLE

When God confronts Cain with his crime, what is his response? "I do not know; am I my brother's keeper?" This is a resounding echo of the excuses of the first father and mother when they are accused by the same God. The Ego is not strong enough to face the consequences of its actions but is clever enough to lie.

As a result of this action, Cain is exiled from his home and condemned to wander the earth. This represents the second stage of the exile from the Garden of Eden. Cain quite rightly objects to this sentence; he knows that it means certain death, because he would be without the protection of his family or, apparently, his God and at the mercy of anyone he encountered:

> Today you have driven me away from the soil, and I shall be hidden from your face; I shall be a fugitive and a wanderer on the earth, and anyone who meets me may kill me.[17]

Cain's plea has an impact on God, who responds by giving him a mark to warn all that "whoever kills Cain will suffer a seven-fold vengeance."[18] Thus the oft-misunderstood Mark of Cain does not condemn him but rather put him under the protection of his God.

The Mark of Cain has its intended effect, as we are told that Cain sets out to the Land of Nod, east of Eden, and settles there successfully. He takes a wife (whom God must have created off stage from our drama), and they conceive and bear sons and descendants who form the

---

17 Genesis 4:14.
18 Genesis 4:15.

beginning of civilization and are the forebears of all who play musical instruments, discoverers of bronze and iron, and those who raise livestock.

This can be seen as a case of the lack of ego-control. It is a very natural thing for someone who does not have self-control to strike out in anger—it is the response of a small child. When children are angry, they will express that anger physically, by hitting a playmate to gain control of a toy that both desire. This action is without control unless imposed by external forces, as the child's or the child's Ego has not developed to the point that the impulses are kept in check.

Here we have both the blessing and curse of God's gift of Ego summed up in a few short verses—the Ego brought the blessing of civilization, which we have been gifted with in the millennia since. It also brought us the heritage of fratricide and murder, resulting from a willingness to act in unimaginable ways to accomplish the ego-based goals. Created in God's image, we have the power to create the world as our Ego believes best.

Chapter 3

Abraham: The Called

> Now the LORD said to Abram, "Go from your country and your kindred and your father's house to the land that I will show you. I will make of you a great nation, and I will bless you, and make your name great, so that you will be a blessing. I will bless those who bless you, and the one who curses you I will curse; and in you all the families of the earth shall be blessed." So Abram went, as the LORD had told him; and Lot went with him. Abram was seventy-five years old when he departed from Haran.[19]

We do not know anything about Abraham (Abram) prior to him receiving the call from Yahweh. This is no simple thing that God commands. Abram is to pick up and leave everything and everyone he knows and go to a land that is a complete mystery to him. Yet there is no indication in the story that Abram hesitates, questions, or demurs at this audacious command from God. There is a promise that goes with the command—one that possibly Abram cannot resist. God promises Abram what men often want even today—to be the father of a great nation. He would be a blessing; God would bless those whom he blesses and curse those he curses. This is a very powerful and dangerous promise. Imagine having God bless all those on your side and, better yet, curse

---
[19] Genesis 12:1–4.

ABRAHAM: THE CALLED

everyone you curse. It seems almost irresistible. Indeed, Abram does not resist—he apparently complies willingly.

These commands from God can be understood in terms of images from the deep unconscious, or the collective unconscious, as Jung named it. These archetypal images are overpowering, as Jung notes:

> That people should succumb to these eternal images is entirely normal, in fact it is what these images are for. They are meant to fascinate and overpower. They are created out of the primal stuff of revelation and reflect the ever-unique experience of divinity.[20]

Abram has an encounter with God—with the Self. Jung famously said that every encounter with the Self (capital S), or the psyche, is a defeat for the Ego. The Self is the centre and totality of the psyche and has been called by Jung the God Image. Abram's Ego certainly here encounters the Self; any resistance he might have felt is overcome. Edward Edinger notes that "the encounter with the Self in indeed a defeat for the ego; but with perseverance, *Deo volente*, light is born from the darkness. One meets the 'immortal One' who wounds and heals, who casts down and raises up, who makes small and makes large—in a word, the One who makes one whole."[21]

Abram's Ego does not appear to have been defeated by this encounter. It appears that God's promise is enough to build up Abram's Ego and assure him that, with God on his side, he is destined for greatness. There

---

20 *The Archetypes of the Collective Unconscious*, 8.
21 *Encounter with the Self*, 9.

THE EGO AND THE BIBLE

is no darkness in this encounter yet, and we shall see that Abram goes on to be wounded by his call and eventually be made whole. Edinger discusses the psychological process involved in Abram's call:

> Psychologically this refers to the separation necessary to break up a state of *participation mystique*. This is a basic requirement of individuation. One must be dumped out of the psychic containers that keep one unconsciously identified with family, tribe, party, church and country. One who succeeds in dissolving this *participation mystique* becomes, like Abraham, a "great nation." To achieve the state of conscious individual being is like the birth of a new world.[22]

Abram sets off on the journey that God has ordained. He encounters his first detour and goes to Egypt, setting a pattern that will be followed by his descendants—the first Joseph, sold into slavery; Jacob's children for the same reason as Abram: famine; and the second Joseph, to escape the wrath of King Herod. Abram, in establishing another family tradition, plays the trickster and passes off Sarai (Sarah) his wife as his sister. The trickster is an image identified by Jung as archetype—energy residing in the collective unconscious of humankind. Jung developed the concept of archetype to represent the structural elements of the psyche which are universal to human beings. The archetypes are structured in factors that people have in common such as mother, father, king, and queen. They are in effect the organizing structures around which the psyche is formed. Jung describes the trickster as "a figure

---

22 *The Bible and the Psyche*, 25.

ABRAHAM: THE CALLED

whose physical appetites dominate his behaviour; he has the mentality of an infant. Lacking any purpose beyond the gratification of his primary needs, he is cruel, cynical, and unfeeling."[23]

Jung also emphasises the unconscious nature of the trickster: "The trickster is a primitive 'cosmic' being of divine-animal nature, on the one hand superior to man because of his superhuman qualities, and on the other hand inferior to him because of his unreason and unconsciousness."[24]

Abram's Ego appears to be fully in control of the situation and is doing whatever it deems necessary to survive, despite the potential negative effect on his wife and the Pharaoh, who—as hard as it is to believe of a ruler in that age, or perhaps any age—is an innocent bystander in this event. Sarai is "taken into the Pharaoh's house" and presumably becomes one of his concubines. Abram is richly rewarded by the Pharaoh, making Abram something of a procurer in today's cultural relativism. However, God seems to have concern for Sarai, even if Abram did not, and afflicts the Pharaoh with "great plagues"—probably impotence, a plague for any ruler in those days or any age.

Abram and Sarai are fortunately, and perhaps surprisingly, treated with deference by the Pharaoh—perhaps as he has concrete evidence that Abram's god was looking out for him. Abram continues on his journey with notable adventures, including receiving a blessing from the priest of the God Most High, Melchizedek, to whom Abram in turn gives a tenth of his possessions, thereby setting the standard for tithing, which

---

23 "Approaching the Unconscious," in *Man and His Symbols*, 103.
24 *The Archetypes of the Collective Unconscious*, 264.

THE EGO AND THE BIBLE

continues today—if more in the breach than in the observance. After this, Abram enters into a covenant with God, who appears to him in a night vision, again promising Abram land and descendants. This time, the Promised Land is specified as the location. Again, there is no indication that Abram's Ego is wounded or transformed by his encounter with the Self, the God Image.

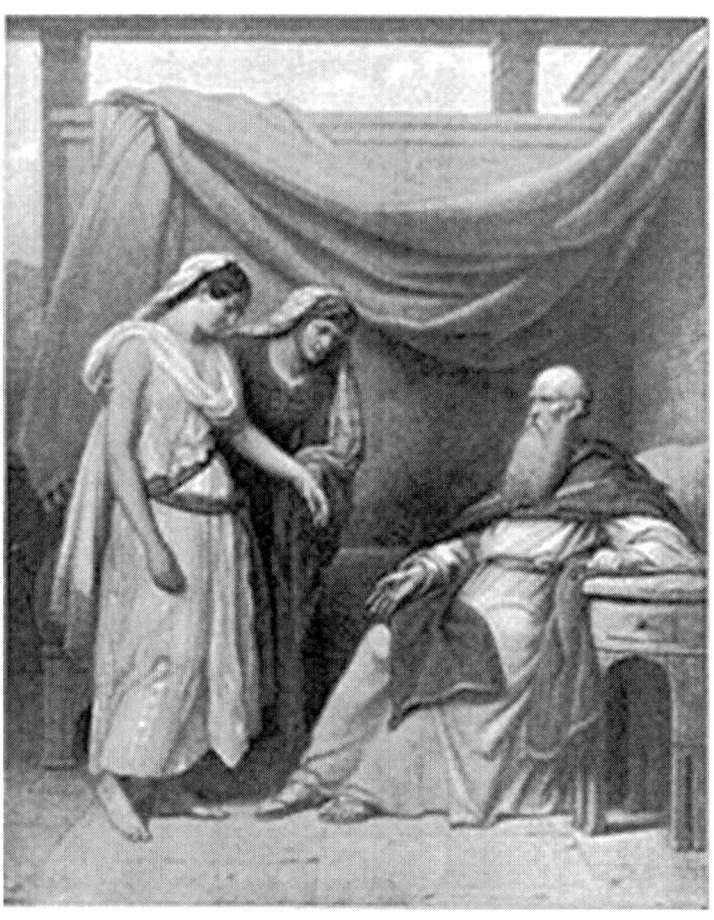

Figure 3 Abraham, Sarah and Hagar

ABRAHAM: THE CALLED

After this encounter, the covenant between Abram and God does not seem to have a possibility of being fulfilled—Sarai bears Abram no children. However, in the established custom, she gives her slave girl Hagar to Abram to try and ensure he will have all-important descendants. This act of Sarai's is seemingly selfless and not Ego centered. Rather it is normal in the cultural tradition of the time. This is not to last long, though, for when Hagar gives Abram his long-desired son, pride and jealousy rear their ugly heads. Hagar conceives and lets her status as mother-to-be of the long-desired son go to her head and looks "with contempt on her mistress." With her pride now ruling, Sarai complains to Abram, and apparently Abram's desire for peace on the family front overcomes his desire to ensure the covenant through the offspring of a slave girl. He places Hagar in Sarai's hands to do with as she will. We are not told what specifically Sarai does to Hagar, but she eventually makes her life so miserable that Hagar runs away into the wilderness. This rash act of Hagar's, which must have meant almost certain death, indicates her lack of Ego control; she lets her emotions loose, and they rule her better judgement.

Just when things look darkest for Hagar and the unborn Ishmael, she has an encounter with an angel of God in the desert. Through the angel, God instructs Hagar to return to her mistress and submit to her, promising that if she does, her offspring will be multitudinous. She comes to her senses—being shocked out of her complex by the encounter—and does as God commands. We do not know if Hagar continues to experience transformation by this encounter with the Self. However, we do know that her Ego is defeated by the encounter, as she apparently is content to live obediently under Sarai's control in the coming years.

THE EGO AND THE BIBLE

God appears to Abram again and renews the covenant. This time, he makes Abram's part of the bargain more specific. It is determined that Abram must institute the ritual of circumcision for himself and all his male offspring as a sign of the covenant. God also commands that Abram and Sarai will from that time forward be named Abraham and Sarah, God again promising that Abraham will be the founder of a great nation through Sarah. Abraham (as he is now known) is rather dubious about God's ability to do this, as he is by now ninety-nine years old. However, he obeys, having himself, Ishmael, and all his male servants circumcised, in accordance with God's will. From this, we can see elements of the transformation that Abraham undergoes thanks to his encounters with the Self. He is willing to submit to the divine will, even though he considers the promise less than realistic.

Abraham goes on to have an adventure that seems to be a regression in his journey—both in terms of events and psychically. Abraham continues on his journey and enters the land of Gerar, which he views with the same apprehension he had experienced upon entering Egypt. He reacts to the perceived danger in an old pattern. He passes off Sarah as his sister, and the king, Abimelech, takes her into his royal household. God again intercedes on behalf of Sarah, warning the king that he was treading unknowingly on the dangerous ground of adultery. This time, God threatens the king with death, rather than a plague. Abraham adds to his complicity by again playing the trickster and trying to use the technicality of language to excuse himself. He claims that Sarah actually is his sister—the daughter of his mother. Again, Abraham comes out of the episode smelling like roses after falling into the dung heap. Abraham is again rewarded richly for his trickery, again for the probable reason that the ruler of the land knows God has Abraham's back. Indeed, he is likely quite glad to see the back of Abraham.

When someone is on a journey of psychic transformation—individuation, as Jung calls it—there is always the danger of regression. The Ego will attempt to reassert itself and sublimate the Self to itself, as happens with Abraham in his encounter with Abimelech. This makes it all the harder for the Ego to surrender its perceived position as the centre of all it surveys. Abraham is rewarded for his trickery and deception, making the Ego even stronger.

Peace reigns with Abraham and Sarah for a few years. Isaac, the long-promised and hoped-for son, is born to Sarah and Abraham. Hagar and Ishmael live as part of this extended family, but unfortunately there is no "happily ever after" in life or in biblical time—except possibly until the Revelation of John comes to fruition. Pride and rivalry rear their ugly heads, and Sarah wants to ensure that Isaac is the only one to inherit. She demands that Abraham cast Hagar and Ishmael into the outer darkness. Abraham does so, on the assurance from God that all would be well. This might be seen as a convenient solution to the domestic dispute. It is convenient when God is seen to do what the Ego wants; however, it is very easy to rationalize the Ego's perspective as being what God also wants. In any case, Abraham is able to carry out Sarah's demand with a clear conscience. However, God's promise regarding Ishmael and Hagar is fulfilled and all was well, at least for the moment.

"After these things God tested Abraham. He said to him, 'Abraham!' And he said, 'Here I am.' He said, 'Take your son, your only son Isaac,

THE EGO AND THE BIBLE

whom you love, and go to the land of Moriah, and offer him there as a burnt-offering on one of the mountains that I shall show you.'"[25]

With these few words, peace no longer reigns for Abraham—God again directly intervenes in Abraham's life. However, this time it is apparently not for Abraham's benefit. As in the case of Job, which we shall explore later, God seems to be putting Abraham to an unnecessary test. Abraham complies with God's seemingly cruel demand without question and sets out to do what might seem to be a dastardly deed. However, in the ultimate act of deus ex machina, God enters at the last moment and stops the sacrificial act. This represents an archetypal act of faithful obedience and surrender by Abraham. Isaac is the fulfilment of the promise in the covenant with God—yet Abraham is willing to put his trust in the divine and subsume all his Ego's desires to be the founder of a great nation.

We must wonder, however, what impact this has on Isaac, who would be at a very impressionable age. Is his trust in God and his father affirmed or shattered? Isaac is not a dominant presence in the story of the patriarchs, and one wonders if he is permanently affected by this event.

---

[25] Genesis 22:1–2.

Chapter 4

Jacob the Trickster

Isaac seems to be blessed with a very uneventful life after the events of the averted sacrifice. He marries and fathers twin sons, Esau, the elder, and Jacob. The twins follow the pattern of their famous twin ancestors, Cain and Abel, in their contentious relationship. As with Cain and Abel, they are very different from each other and their lives are destined to take different courses. This pattern is established from the time they were in the womb:

> And the Lord said to her, "Two nations are in your womb, and two peoples born of you shall be divided; one shall be stronger than the other, the elder shall serve the younger."
>
> When her time to give birth was at hand, there were twins in her womb.
>
> The first came out red, all his body like a hairy mantle; so they named him Esau.
>
> Afterwards his brother came out, with his hand gripping Esau's heel; so he was named Jacob. Isaac was sixty years old when she bore them.[26]

---
26 Genesis 25:23–26.

Esau grows to be the quintessential "man's man"—he is a hunter and a man of the field. Jacob, on the other hand, is a quiet man who sticks to the tents. Tellingly, we are informed that Rebekah, their mother, loves Jacob, who could be described as a momma's boy. Isaac loves Esau because Isaac "was fond of game"; he apparently also loves what Esau could do for him. However, we are not told how Isaac felt about Jacob.

The first major event that shows the truth of God's testament occurs when Esau, coming from a day of hard work and famished, impulsively sells his birthright for a "mess of pottage" that Jacob has prepared. Jacob cleverly demands this as payment for providing the sustenance. Esau, the impulsive one, does not consider the long-term consequences—he is ruled by his feelings rather than by his rational nature. Jacob shows that he is the one who can plan ahead and is able to read the nature of his twin brother. He also shows evidence of being under the influence of the trickster archetype that is, first, part of his ancestor Cain's personality and, later, an aspect of the patriarch Abraham. This trait will develop as events in his life unfold in the near future. Isaac also displays this characteristic by pulling the same trick on poor Abimelech as his father had. He too passes off his wife, Rebekah, as his sister. Abimelech is once more duped into taking the wife/sister into his entourage. However, this time the subterfuge is discovered when Isaac is observed "fondling his wife." Again, the result of this trickery is nothing but beneficial to the biblical patriarch, and Abimelech issues an order protecting Rebekah and, by association, Isaac.

JACOB THE TRICKSTER

Jacob again is energized by the trickster archetype when he is encouraged by his mother to steal Esau's blessing from their father, Isaac. Jacob disguises himself as Esau and so gains Isaac's blessing. Poor stolid, unimaginative Esau is not blessed with either the energy of the archetype or the father's blessing due the firstborn, and he is quite rightly enraged by Jacob's trickery. Isaac has no blessing for Esau, who will be destined to live an uneventful life—unlike Jacob, who is at that point on the run from his brother's wrath. Perhaps there is a blessing for Esau after all—the peace and tranquillity of a quiet life.

Jacob, however, is not to be blessed this way; rather, he will be blessed to live in interesting times. While on his way to his uncle Laban's home, he experiences his first encounter with the divine—and what an encounter it is. One night, he has his famous dream of the ladder between earth and heaven on which angels ascend and descend. Knowing, as people in those days did, that dreams are often from God, he realizes that this place where he laid his head is "the gate of heaven." In response to his divine intercession, he uses the rock that had been his pillow as a pillar and anointed it with oil as a holy place.

THE EGO AND THE BIBLE

Figure 4 Jacob's Ladder

At this point, Jacob acknowledges God, but he makes the mistake of bargaining with God:

> Then Jacob made a vow, saying, "If God will be with me, and will keep me in this way that I go, and will give me

JACOB THE TRICKSTER

> bread to eat and clothing to wear, so that I come again to my father's house in peace, then the LORD shall be my God, and this stone, which I have set up for a pillar, shall be God's house; and of all that you give me I will surely give one-tenth to you."[27]

This attempt by Jacob to bargain with the divine shows that his Ego still believes it is the centre of the world and can control everything—even the divine will. He is not yet defeated by his encounter with the Self and is not yet prepared for that part of the encounter that still lies ahead of him.

Jacob journeys on and is welcomed warmly into his uncle Laban's household. Laban determines that because Jacob is kin, he should serve him for nothing. This should be a red flag to Jacob that Laban is also a shrewd man and not to be trusted. However, they bargain and settle on the agreement that he will serve Laban for seven years to gain Laban's daughter Rachel for his wife. Jacob faithfully fulfills his part of the bargain. However, Laban shows his true colours by tricking Jacob and substituting his older daughter, Leah, in place of the more beautiful Rachel, in the wedding ceremony. Laban shows that he can be possessed by trickster energy, and the trickster Jacob is the one who was tricked. He shows the full extent of this archetypal energy by his bold-face declaration that he is quite justified in this deceit: "This is not done in our country—giving the younger before the firstborn."[28]

The difference between Leah and Rachel is not elaborated on in the story. However, we are told that "Leah's eyes were lovely, and Rachel was

---

27 Genesis 28:20–22.
28 Genesis 29:26.

THE EGO AND THE BIBLE

graceful and beautiful." She appears to be damned with faint praise. It is Rachel whom Jacob loves; so he says, "I will serve you seven years for your younger daughter Rachel."[29] Rachel carries the image of Jacob's anima—his feminine archetype in his unconscious. Therefore, he was willing to do whatever was necessary to possess her. Poor Leah is destined to live in a loveless marriage, despite God's help in giving her sons:

> When the LORD saw that Leah was unloved, he opened her womb; but Rachel was barren. Leah conceived and bore a son, and she named him Reuben; for she said, "Because the LORD has looked on my affliction; surely now my husband will love me."[30]

However, that is not to be. Although Rachel is loved by Jacob, she is no happier than her sister Leah, whom Jacob does not love:

> When Rachel saw that she bore Jacob no children, she envied her sister; and she said to Jacob, "Give me children, or I shall *die!*" Jacob became very angry with Rachel and said, "Am I in the place of God, who has withheld from you the fruit of the womb?" Then she said, "Here is my maid Bilhah; go in to her, that she may bear upon my knees and that I too may have children through her." So she gave him her maid Bilhah as a wife; and Jacob went in to her. And Bilhah conceived and bore Jacob a son.[31]

---

29 Genesis 29:17–18.
30 Genesis 29:3–32.
31 Genesis 30:1–4.

As this passage shows, Rachel is desperate to bear Jacob a son and is jealous of Leah, who has by then borne Jacob four sons. Desperate enough to follow the family tradition, she gives her maid Bilhah to Jacob as his concubine. Bilhah, a dutiful handmaiden, duly gives Jacob two sons. Leah, not to be outdone in the competition between the sisters, offers her maid Zilpah to Jacob, and Zilpah bears him two sons. The competition continues until Jacob has ten sons. However, Rachel, the love of his life, is still barren. God finally "remembers" Rachel and gives her a son, Joseph, to make the count eleven.

Jacob at that point decides it is time to return to his home. Laban agrees, even acknowledging that he has been blessed by God and prospered because of Jacob. He proposes that Jacob name his own wages for having served Laban. Jacob proposes this: "Let me pass through all your flock today, removing from it every speckled and spotted sheep and every black lamb, and the spotted and speckled among the goats; and such shall be my wages."[32] Laban's generous offering is not what it seems—his nature runs true to course as he attempts to ensure that Jacob does not receive his due. Laban removes all the goats and sets "a distance of three days" journey between them and Jacob. However, Jacob is not to be outdone in this—he proves to be a better trickster than Laban, using sympathetic magic to have the flock produce offspring that are "striped, speckled and spotted."

This produces for Jacob not only riches but also Laban's enmity. God again intercedes on Jacob's behalf, advising Jacob to return to his home and promising to be with him. Jacob tells his wives that God ordained

---

32 Genesis 30:32.

all that has happened when Jacob tricked Laban to gain the wages he deserved. Jacob then steals away with all his family and his possessions with the intent of returning to his home. Rachel also steals Laban's household gods (Teraphim). This rather curious act is not explained. There are various possibilities: perhaps she wants them because she is used to worshipping them; she may also want them as a source of divination to determine the best way to escape Laban's pursuit. It could also be that she does not want her father to use them as a source of divination to pursue them successfully. In any case, Jacob, for once, is not behind the trickery and is truly unaware that Rachel has done this. In all this, Jacob shows that he does not truly believe that God is on his side. He believes that he must use trickery and deception—even with his wives—to get what he desires. His Ego is still in control and has not been defeated by all his encounters with the Self.

Laban pursues Jacob, but again God intercedes and sends Laban a dream warning him not to harm Jacob. Laban pays attention to this warning but is angry at the theft of the Teraphim and searches the camp. Rachel shows herself a worthy wife to Jacob, using trickery to hide the gods under her saddle and then excusing herself from rising in her father's presence because "the way of women is upon me." Laban seems to know that he has met his match in Jacob, and so he makes a covenant with him. Laban then departs in peace, and Jacob is allowed to continue on his way.

When Jacob approaches Esau's location he is understandably wary that Esau will still carry a deep grudge against him for his trickery. He is afraid that Esau will take fatal revenge against him; therefore, he takes precautions and calls on God to protect him. He does not leave it to

God alone but sends presents to Esau. Facing an existential crisis, Jacob awaits the encounter with Esau with dread.

In this crisis, Jacob is visited again by the divine—he encounters a man who turns out to be an angel of the Lord. Jacob engages the angel in a literal wrestling match. The encounter becomes a marathon match which carries on until dawn. Interestingly, the angel is concerned when day breaks. Jacob demands a blessing to release him, and he receives a blessing from the angel and a new name, Israel, as a result of the encounter:

> When the man saw that he did not prevail against Jacob, he struck him on the hip socket; and Jacob's hip was put out of joint as he wrestled with him. Then he said, "Let me go, for the day is breaking." But Jacob said, "I will not let you go, unless you bless me." So he said to him, "What is your name?" And he said, "Jacob." Then the man said, "You shall no longer be called Jacob, but Israel, for you have striven with God and with humans, and have prevailed." Then Jacob asked him, "Please tell me your name." But he said, "Why is it that you ask my name?" And there he blessed him. So Jacob called the place Peniel, saying, "For I have seen God face to face, and yet my life is preserved." The sun rose upon him as he passed Peniel, limping because of his hip. Therefore to this day the Israelites do not eat the thigh muscle that is on the hip socket, because he struck Jacob on the hip socket at the thigh muscle.[33]

---

[33] Genesis 32:25–32.

THE EGO AND THE BIBLE

This time, he is transformed by his encounter with the Self—not only does he have a new name but he is also permanently affected physically. No one can encounter the Self as Jacob does and ultimately not be changed. The Ego of anyone in such a situation will be defeated. Jacob limps away a new man to meet his twin, Esau.

Charles Williams notes that there are three degrees of consciousness: the old self on the old way, the old self on the new way, and the new self on the new way:

> The second group is the largest at all times and in all places…it forms…at most moments practically all of oneself that one can know, for the new self does not know itself. It consists of the existence of the self, unselfish perhaps, but not yet denied. This self often applies itself unselfishly. It transfers its activities from itself unselfishly as a centre to its belief as a centre. It uses its anger on behalf of its religion or its morals, and its greed and its fear and its pride. It operates on behalf of its notion of God as it originally operated on behalf of itself. It aims honestly at better behaviour, but it does not usually aim at change.[34]

We do not know if Jacob is a new Self in the old way that clings to the familiar in an old way. He may indeed be one of those few who is truly transformed and is now a new self on a new way.

---

34 Charles Williams, *He Came Down From Heaven* (London: Faber and Faber), 85.

Jacob ultimately returns at God's command to Bethel, where he had encountered the ladder between heaven and earth at the beginning of his journey of transformation. God appears to him one final time and confirms he is at that point Israel, who will father "a company of nations" and will receive the land that God gave to Abraham and Isaac. As confirmation of this blessing, Rachel gives birth to Jacob's last and most beloved son, Benjamin—"the son of the right hand." His sons now number twelve—twelve tribes which will constitute the nation of Israel.

Chapter 5

Joseph the Dreamer

> Jacob settled in the land where his father had lived as an alien, the land of Canaan. This is the story of the family of Jacob. Joseph, being seventeen years old, was shepherding the flock with his brothers; he was a helper to the sons of Bilhah and Zilpah, his father's wives; and Joseph brought a bad report of them to their father. Now Israel loved Joseph more than any other of his children, because he was the son of his old age; and he had made him a long robe with sleeves. But when his brothers saw that their father loved him more than all his brothers, they hated him, and could not speak peaceably to him.[35]

The myth of Joseph and his brothers is a story of the blessing and curse of the Ego, which is made manifest in many of the different characters in the story—both great and small. Joseph has been blessed by God, apparently from his earliest years, with the gift of dreams—initially as one who had prophetic dreams and later as one who would understand their meaning. As we shall see, this is both a blessing and an apparent curse.

The Ego first exerts itself in Joseph's story when he is seventeen, and it involves not Joseph's Ego but that of his father, Jacob. Jacob shows

---

[35] Genesis 37:1–4.

favouritism toward Joseph—the first son of his favoured wife, Rachel—and gives him a long coat with sleeves (otherwise known as a coat of many colours). Jacob allows his preference for Joseph to be expressed without using his Ego to exercise judgement; this means he fails to consider how this would affect either Joseph or his brothers. Now, this must be considered in the context of the times—the patriarch can act as he wishes with few of the constraints of our times. However, from our context, it is helpful to reflect upon this wilfulness and see how our Egos can constrain us or not.

This action is not well received by the brothers, and we are told that "they hated him and could not speak peaceably with him." Here we see another aspect of lack of Ego control. The brothers are unable to overcome their resentment and treat Joseph, if not with brotherly love, at least civilly. As we shall see, this resentment and the hurt Egos will shortly bloom into action.

> Once Joseph had a dream, and when he told it to his brothers, they hated him even more. He said to them, "Listen to this dream that I dreamed. There we were, binding sheaves in the field. Suddenly my sheaf rose and stood upright; then your sheaves gathered around it, and bowed down to my sheaf." His brothers said to him, "Are you indeed to reign over us? Are you indeed to have dominion over us?" So they hated him even more because of his dreams and his words.[36]

---

36 Genesis 37:5–8.

THE EGO AND THE BIBLE

At this point, Joseph receives a dream—or rather two prophetic dreams. In the first, he and his brothers are binding sheaves of wheat, and the brothers' sheaves bow down to Joseph's. Joseph, being full of himself, thanks to his father's favouritism—or perhaps because of God's intentions—tells his brothers about his marvellous dream. Well, of course his brothers, who already resent him, do not take well this apparent foretelling of further insult added to their present injury. However, they hold their feelings in check and do not act on them—at least for now.

Joseph then has another dream, one in which not only the brothers—as represented by stars—but also his father and mother—represented by the sun and moon—bow down to Joseph. This time, even his father rebukes him for this rashness. Joseph's Ego is now inflated about as much as is humanly possible. He is ripe for the fall that follows.

When the opportunity presents itself, the brothers act on their resentment and hatred, selling Joseph into what will be slavery in Egypt. It would have been a sentence of death rather than mere slavery if his brother Reuben had not used his Ego to control his emotions and persuaded the brothers to be '"merciful" by selling him into slavery, intending later to set him free before they could accomplish this. However, the brothers, not to have their revenge thwarted, sell him into slavery without Reuben's knowledge. The hurt Egos of the brothers are salved—at least for the present moment.

Joseph's inflated Ego is at that point punctured in the worst way imaginable. From being the apple of his father's eye, who strutted around in his coat with sleeves, lording it over his brothers, he becomes the lowliest of the low—a slave with a very uncertain future. Certainly, it appears there is no way that his dreams of greatness can come to fruition. However, Joseph's prospects take an unexpected turn for the better. Against all expectations, his position—and probably his spirit as well—are raised to unexpected heights. He finds favour with his master, Potiphar, and is placed in an important position in his master's house. We can see a glimmer of possibility that his prophetic dreams of greatness may yet come to fruition. However, Ego arises with its ugly aspect in full force.

While the cat is away, the mouse—in this case, Potiphar's wife—sees an opportunity to play; she lets her desires rule her actions. Her Ego sees no reason why she can't have what she desires, and so she propositions Joseph. However, Joseph shows better Ego control than in the past and refuses the probably tempting offer. Here we see that Joseph has gained Ego control, learning from his experience. However, hell hath no fury as Potiphar's wife scorned, and Joseph ends up back in prison when Potiphar choose the safer course and listens to his wife's version of events, perhaps believing that he would have yielded to the temptation that his wife presented if he were in Joseph's position.

Figure 5 Joseph and Potiphar's Wife, Joseph leaving

Things again look grim for Joseph. However, God's grace once again shines upon him, and he finds favour with the chief jailer, who puts him in charge of the other prisoners. We now begin to believe that there is a real possibility for Joseph's prophetic dreams to come to fruition. Two of the prisoners in Joseph's care—the Pharaoh's cup bearer and the Pharaoh's chief baker, both of whom have fallen from the Pharaoh's favour—have dreams. Joseph uses the gift God has blessed him with and interprets these dreams. Here again, we see that Joseph benefits from the slings and arrows that have assailed him. He learns to use the gift for the benefit of others rather than for self-aggrandizement. He has matured to the extent that he is no longer concerned only with gratifying his Ego.

Joseph's ability to interpret dreams is now verified and his understanding of the two dreams fulfilled—to the joy of the cup bearer, who is restored to his former position, and the sorrow of the chief baker, who literally loses his head. Again, Joseph shows that he has learned from his experiences. Rather than letting the success of his venture into dream interpretation go to his head, which would surely result in greater inflation, he gives the credit where it belongs: "Do not interpretations belong to God?"[37] This probably makes his disappointment bearable when the promise of the cup bearer—to mention him to the Pharaoh—is forgotten. God's gift of dream interpretation begins to truly stand Joseph in good stead. The Pharaoh dreams two dreams (a significant repetition of a motif that Joseph understands to mean that God's intention is fixed), which no one in the kingdom is able to interpret. Fortunately the cup bearer remembers Joseph, who is brought to the Pharaoh's court. Joseph reveals to the Pharaoh the message that God has for him, predicting seven years of plenty followed by seven years of famine. Joseph advises the Pharaoh to appoint a wise and discerning man to handle the coming crisis. The Pharaoh wisely chooses Joseph for this important task. There is a hint that Joseph's Ego encourages him to make this suggestion unasked—who better to handle the consequences of the prediction than the one who predicted it? However, Joseph likely realistically assessed his own ability; he may have been confident that this was part of God's master plan, which was now coming to fruition.

In due course, as was part of God's plan, Joseph's brothers (minus Benjamin) come to Egypt, seeking relief from the famine that now plagues the world. They appear before Joseph and bow down to him, thus fulfilling Joseph's first dream, in which the brothers' sheaves bow to his sheaf. Joseph does not reveal himself to them but acts harshly and tricks them, forcing them to bring his full brother, Benjamin, to Egypt.

---

37 Genesis 40:8b.

The question arises as to why Joseph would not just reveal himself and have a happy reunion with his long-separated brothers. It would hardly be surprising if he had succumbed to the Ego's desire for payback and made his brothers suffer for their evil deeds. However, this would be out of character, as Joseph seems to have matured to the point of no longer allowing his Ego to dictate his actions.

Joseph must have known the distress that his action—demanding Benjamin be brought to Egypt—would have caused his father. So, why did he take this action? I believe that his actions were necessary for there to be true reconciliation between Joseph and his brothers and his father. If Joseph had immediately identified himself and welcomed them with open arms, there would have always been a barrier between the brothers and him, and perhaps between the brothers and their father. They would have always wondered if Joseph had truly forgiven them, and, with the Egos they had, they might eventually have—secretly or not so secretly—resented his good fortune in Egypt, just as they had resented the dreams that foretold these events.

Jacob's Ego now comes into play in a major way. He refuses to let the brothers take Benjamin—the remaining son of his true love, Rachel—despite Reuben's surprising promise to give his two sons' lives as security for Benjamin's return. His desire to keep the possession dearest to him outweighs any consideration for the life of his son Simeon, who is being held in Egypt as surety for their return. The Ego wants what it wants, regardless of other consequences.

Finally, famine forces Jacob to relent and allow Benjamin to accompany the brothers to Egypt. Again, Joseph uses trickery to test his brothers as he threatens to keep Benjamin as a slave—much to the consternation of the brothers, for they fear their father would not survive such a disaster. At this point, Judah steps up and requests that he be allowed to take Benjamin's place. This is a true act of heroism, as he is willing to sacrifice himself for the sake of his father. As with all acts of true heroism, the natural impulse of the Ego for self-preservation is overcome by a higher principle and becomes willing to risk annihilation. This self-sacrificing act by Judah, which is out of character from his earlier attitude, is the surrender of the Ego to the higher principle. It is by this act that Joseph knows that it is now safe to reveal himself to his brothers.

In a footnote to the story, we hear of the acts of Joseph in respect to the people of Egypt. With the famine still raging throughout the land, the people eventually sell all they possess—their livestock as well as their land—to Joseph, and when that money is gone, they sell themselves to the Pharaoh as slaves. This seems to be heartless and out of character on the part of Joseph as the Pharaoh's representative. However, there is an element of a fable in this add-on to the story. It is used to explain how the Pharaoh came to own all the land in Egypt. However, it also shows Joseph's wisdom in terms of the arrangement:

> Then Joseph said to the people, "Now that I have this day bought you and your land for Pharaoh, here is seed for you; sow the land. And at the harvests you shall give one-fifth to Pharaoh, and four-fifths shall be your own, as seed for the field and as food for yourselves and your households, and as food for your little ones." They said, "You have saved our lives; may it please my lord, we will be slaves to Pharaoh." So Joseph made it

> a statute concerning the land of Egypt, and it stands to this day, that Pharaoh should have the fifth. The land of the priests alone did not become Pharaoh's.[38]

The story of Joseph has a happy ending—you could almost think they lived happily ever after, with Jacob settling in Egypt and living out his days there. However, as in life, happily ever after only lasts for so long in the Bible—at least until the Revelation which is yet to come. We shall see what happens to the descendants of Joseph next.

---

[38] Genesis 47:23–26.

Chapter 6

Moses the Law Giver

Now a man from the house of Levi went and married a Levite woman. The woman conceived and bore a son; and when she saw that he was a fine baby, she hid him for three months. When she could hide him no longer she got a papyrus basket for him, and plastered it with bitumen and pitch; she put the child in it and placed it among the reeds on the bank of the river. His sister stood at a distance, to see what would happen to him. The daughter of Pharaoh came down to bathe at the river, while her attendants walked beside the river. She saw the basket among the reeds and sent her maid to bring it.[39]

Figure 6 Moses rescued from the Nile.

---

39 Exodus 2:1–5.

THE EGO AND THE BIBLE

Moses's birth is one of a mythic hero. He is twice born; being of lowly birth, he is set adrift on the water and drawn out of the water into a new life with new parents. He is raised as the Pharaoh's son. As we shall see, he will receive a divine call and do wondrous deeds. Moses lives the hero's life, but it is also one in which Ego plays a significant role.

At this point, a new Pharaoh has become ruler in Egypt—one who has forgotten Joseph and enslaves the Israelites. Despite his best or worst efforts, the Israelites become more and more numerous in slavery.

As the Ego always fears loss of control, so the Egyptians begin to fear the Israelites. The Pharaoh issues an edict that all boy children born to the Israelites are to be killed. However, such attempts to control can only succeed for so long. In this case, it will inevitably lead to the defeat they are trying to prevent. To prevent his death, Moses's mother sets him adrift in the Nile, where fate or God intercedes. He is discovered by the Pharaoh's daughter, who raises him as her own son.

The first thing we learn about Moses, after the events surrounding his birth, is that he kills an Egyptian overseer who was beating "one of his kinsfolk," although we are not told how he learns of his heritage. This outburst of righteous anger is not entirely uncontrolled, though; we are told, "He looked this way and that, and seeing no one he killed the Egyptian and hid him in the sand."[40] This calculating step means that he is committing premeditated murder rather than manslaughter—it is an act of the Ego asserting itself.

---

40   Exodus 2:12.

MOSES THE LAW GIVER

Despite his efforts at deception, Moses's criminal act is discovered, and he flees to the land of Median, where he marries one of the daughters of the priest of Median and has a son, settling into what might have been a quiet life as a shepherd. However, the gods—or in this case God—has other plans for him.

> Moses was keeping the flock of his father-in-law Jethro, the priest of Midian; he led his flock beyond the wilderness, and came to Horeb, the mountain of God. There the angel of the LORD appeared to him in a flame of fire out of a bush; he looked, and the bush was blazing, yet it was not consumed.[41]

Moses encounters God in the burning bush and sets the next chapter of his destiny in motion. His mission impossible—should he accept it—is to lead the Israelites out of slavery to freedom. However, Moses, because of his Ego, is reluctant to accept this daunting task. Yet once he is assured that God will be with him in his task and provides him with miraculous powers, he accepts it.

As noted above, Jung famously said that every encounter with the Self is a defeat for the Ego. The Self is the centre and totality of the psyche and has been called by Jung the God Image. Moses's Ego here certainly encounters the Self, in the burning bush, and his resistance is overcome. Edward Edinger notes that "the encounter with the Self is indeed a defeat for the ego; but with perseverance, Deo volente, light is born from the darkness."[42] When the Ego does not resist the Self, but rather

---
41 Genesis 3:1–2.
42 *Encounter with the Self.*

THE EGO AND THE BIBLE

cooperates with it, miraculous things can happen—perhaps not as wonderful as those that happened with Moses, but we can do things that would otherwise be beyond what the Ego can do by itself.

Moses comes to Egypt and demands that the Israelites be released from slavery. The Pharaoh's reaction is predictable—whenever the Ego is threatened, its reaction is to do the same thing only harder. The Pharaoh increases the hardships for the Israelites, making them produce bricks without straw. The Israelites, in turn, want someone to blame for their hardship—in this case, Moses—rather than the true cause—their slave masters and, ultimately, the Pharaoh. This pattern will be repeated many times throughout Moses's story. The Pharaoh will resist the persistent demands to release the Israelites. The efforts of Moses—through miraculous deeds with Aaron's rod and the plagues that God sends on the Egyptians—are challenged in a game of "anything you can do I can do better." The plagues sent by God on the Egyptians are ignored by the Pharaoh, if not the Egyptian people, until he receives a blow that overpowers his resistance—the death of his son. The final plague is the death of all of Egypt's firstborn except those "passed over" because of the protection of the sign of blood on the doorposts of the houses of the Israelites.

The Ego of the Pharaoh does not give up easily. An Ego wants above all to be in control and will resist a challenge to its predominance—particularly if it is inflated by power. The Pharaoh is particularly vulnerable to having an inflated Ego. The Pharaoh rules with absolute control over the people of his country. Indeed, his position, as the absolute ruler of Egypt, is literally that of a god. He cannot relinquish the power that comes with the position until he is defeated by a greater power in a way he cannot ignore—the death of his son and heir. Even after this defeat, his Ego will not surrender absolutely. It exerts itself and tries to gain back what he has lost by pursuing the Israelites as they are leaving captivity in Egypt. The Pharaoh meets his ultimate defeat in the waters of the Red Sea. His power is overcome and drowned, an appropriate symbol for the Ego being engulfed by the power of the unconscious. The Pharaoh's Ego has encountered the Self and been truly defeated—a defeat from which he will not recover, as his persona—a God Image to all of Egypt, including himself—cannot submit to the absolute God Image.

When the Israelites blame Moses for their increased workload, it is not the last time they seek to shift the blame to a convenient—if not safe—scapegoat. They will blame Moses for leading them into the wilderness, where there is hardship and death around the next corner. They yearn for the fleshpots of Egypt, where they had security, if not freedom. The Ego will seek the grass that seems greener and the life that is easier or more secure. When the Ego is seeking to satisfy itself rather than seeking meaning from the divine, it is never satisfied. It will seek manna when it is hungry, but even bread from heaven will seem to be inadequate, and then rather than manna it will seek meat. The Israelites blame Moses when there is no water to drink, rather than taking responsibility for their decision to escape slavery for the Promised Land. As with the example of the Israelites, the Ego must realize that it is not the centre of the world if it is to take responsibility for the decisions that it has made.

Moses encounters God again. This time, it is not a voice in a burning bush. Moses encounters the divine presence where it so often seems to manifest itself—on a mountain top. Moses encounters God on Mount

THE EGO AND THE BIBLE

Sinai and receives the epiphany of the divine law—tablets with the Ten Commandments. This appears to be a perfect encounter between the Ego and the Self. Moses's faithfulness is rewarded with the divine gift of the Law, according to which the people can contain the desires of their Egos. With the divine law to keep the devices and desires of their hearts under wraps—if not controlled—all should now go as Moses and God intend. However, this perfect peace is not to be.

While Moses is communing with God, the Israelites grow restless and, under Aaron's direction, create an idol to worship. Here we have a variation on the desire of the Ego for security. They want a god to worship and to give them what they want. It is a case of "what have Moses and his God done for us lately?" They want a god that they can bring out and put away on demand, which will give them what they want without any question. This has been brilliantly described elsewhere as "God the butler."[43] God the butler can be called up from the basement quarters to provide the things that will satisfy our Egos' desires.

At this point in the story, it is almost as though God's Ego comes into play. God is enraged by the faithlessness of the people he has led out of slavery. If God could be said to have an Ego—that image of God we were created in—God's pride seems to have been injured. He declares to Moses, "I have seen this people, how stiff-necked they are. Now let me alone, so that my wrath may burn hot against them and I may consume them; and of you I will make a great nation."[44]

---

43 The expression was used by Miroslav Volf in a lecture at Regis College in Toronto in 2013.
44 Exodus 32:9–10.

Moses now takes what seems to be the mature approach and convinces God to have mercy on his wayward people. He reminds God, who seems to have put aside his omniscience for the moment, of his covenant with Abraham and his descendants, reasoning with God that it would be better to forgive them than start again with a new people to fulfil that covenant. Now that God's wrath is placated and He has changed His mind, Moses returns, carrying the tablets of the Law, to the recalcitrant Israelites. Upon finding the people revelling in their joy of having a new god to worship, he is now the one who is burning with righteous wrath. He breaks the tablets in an act of uncontrolled rage. When Moses confronts Aaron regarding the sinfulness of the people, Aaron does not take responsibility for the idolatry, claiming to not know how this golden image could have come to be, "So I said to them, 'Whoever has gold, take it off'; so they gave it to me, and I threw it into the fire, and out came this calf!"[45] Here we have again the desire by the Ego to avoid responsibility for decisions. It harkens back to the precedent established by the first parents—Adam saying Eve gave him the apple and Eve saying the serpent made her do it.

Unfortunately for the recalcitrant Israelites, Moses does not have a Moses to convince him not to act on his wrath. On his orders, three thousand Israelites meet their maker that day. I wonder if God had any qualms about Moses taking action that God himself had threatened. Moses demonstrates his lack of consciousness and Ego control in acting upon his wrath. However, this does not stand in the way of

---

45 Exodus 32:24.

his relationship with God. Moses again ascends Mount Sinai to receive a duplicate copy of the tablets. He remains on the mountain for the significant period that often results in transformations—forty days and forty nights. When he returns, he has been transformed by the encounter with the divine—the Self. That transformation now shows through, with the inner light he now possesses or is now possessed by shining forth for all to behold. This is the outward manifestation of an inner radiance resulting from the Ego's encounter and incorporation with the Self. Moses is no longer under the control of his Ego—the Ego is now in service to the Self.

Moses is now at a state of development or individuation, as Jung calls it, where he has reached the border of the Promised Land. He goes to the top of Mount Pisgah, where God shows him the Promised Land. However, God will not let Moses cross over to the destination to which he has led his people. It may seem strange that God would deny Moses this ultimate fulfilment after the journey that he has given his all to complete. To be given a glimpse and then have it denied to him seems cruel. However, this is viewed from the position of our Egos. We believe that we should be rewarded with our heart's desire if we put everything into it. Did not Moses do everything that was asked of him? There was his sin at the waters of Meribah, which sin was not trusting in God and instead falling back on his own efforts.[46] However, this seems to be a trivial matter, to our eyes, especially in light of such a severe punishment. I believe that Moses is now in a state where his Ego is completely subsumed by the Self. He has

---

46 Numbers 20:12.

reached the end of his journey of individuation, and there is no need for the Ego's goals to be fulfilled. In effect, his Ego has reached this psychic Promised Land, and there is no necessity, or even desire, to enter the literal one.

Chapter 7

Samson the Blind Hero

> The Israelites again did what was evil in the sight of the Lord, and the Lord gave them into the hand of the Philistines for forty years. There was a certain man of Zorah, of the tribe of the Danites, whose name was Manoah. His wife was barren, having borne no children. And the angel of the Lord appeared to the woman and said to her, "Although you are barren, having borne no children, you shall conceive and bear a son. Now be careful not to drink wine or strong drink, or to eat anything unclean, for you shall conceive and bear a son. No razor is to come on his head, for the boy shall be a nazarite to God from birth. It is he who shall begin to deliver Israel from the hand of the Philistines."[47]

The story of Samson begins with the Israelites in thrall, again, to a foreign power. This time, they are under the rule of a people destined to be their nemeses for many years—the Philistines. This happens because they "again did evil in the sight of the Lord." Whenever people, or an individual, follow the devices and desires of their Egos, they fall into trouble. When this happens, we will look for someone or something to rescue us. We believe that all will be well if we have a strong leader

---
47 Judges 13:1–5.

to solve all our problems. This is the attitude of the child who wants the parent to rescue them. For a child who has not yet developed Ego strength, this is appropriate; however, for an adult individual or a people, it is the sign of an Ego that needs to develop and mature. As with the Israelites in Egypt, God hears their cries and sends them a hero.

As with the story of many heroes, we hear of Samson's miraculous birth. It is announced by a messenger from God, who foretells that he will release the Israelites from captivity. However, unlike many heroes' stories, we hear little or nothing of his childhood. Samson bursts onto the scene being possessed by a case of love at first sight. He has been captured by his anima—the inner feminine in his psyche. We are told by Samson that it was ordained by God that he should have this Philistine woman as his wife, giving Samson a pretext to act against the Philistines as they had "dominion over the Israelites."[48] However, this does not ring true, as Samson does not yet have the judgement to carry out such a plan—whether ordained by God or not.

Jung notes that with the anima, "we enter the realms of the gods, or rather, the realm that metaphysics has reserved for itself."[49] Jung further elaborates that, as with all energy in the unconscious, the anima has both a positive and negative aspect. "Because the anima wants life, she wants both good and bad."[50]

In Samson's case, unfortunately, the anima manifests in its negative aspect. Samson acts with the impetuousness and rashness of someone

---
48 Judges 14:4.
49 *The Archetypes and the Collective Unconscious*, 28.
50 Ibid.

THE EGO AND THE BIBLE

who believes he can gain whatever his heart desires. He has been given the attributes of a hero—great strength and an impulse toward action; however, his abilities have gone to his head. His Ego has been inflated, which will cause him to follow the hubris of those who believe they are invincible and which is always a precursor to a fall. Jung held that the Ego can respond to the Self in two ways—either being subsumed by it or assimilating it, as noted by Faith Luton, a Jungian analyst:

> Identification with the self can manifest in two ways: the assimilation of the Ego by the self, in which case the Ego falls under the control of the unconscious; or the assimilation of the self to the Ego, where the Ego becomes over accentuated. In both cases the result is inflation, with disturbances in adaptation.[51]

His rashness and his desire to possess his anima are shown in his relationships with, first, his wife and, later, the infamous Delilah. He reveals his secrets to both and they both in turn betray him. Rather than him possessing his anima, it possesses him. Initially his wife, whom he has just married, reveals the secret of the riddle that is the basis of a bet with his wedding guests:

> He said to them,
> "Out of the eater came something to eat.
> Out of the strong came something sweet."
> But for three days they could not explain the riddle.[52]

---

51 http://frithluton.com/articles/ego/
52 Judges 14:14.

Samson is enraged by this betrayal of his wife, and in response he kills thirty Philistine men. The Philistines in turn take his wife from him and give her to the Philistine who had served as his best man. This gives him the excuse, as if he needed one, to wage warfare against the Philistines. It is actually terrorism more than war. The Philistines again seek to use Samson's weakness for the feminine and have Delilah, the new outer representation of his anima, to find the secret of his strength. She betrays him three times, and yet he finally reveals to her the secret of his superhuman strength: "A razor has never come upon my head; for I have been a nazarite to God from my mother's womb."[53]

Samson discovers that he has indeed been betrayed, and that he is indeed not invincible. The balloon of his inflated Ego has now burst, and the fall that follows matches the great heights to which it had risen. He is captured by the enemies of the Israelites—the Philistines—and his eyes are put out. The loss of his eyesight symbolically represents the blindness with which he has lived his life up to this point—being blinded by the possession of his anima and the inflation of his Ego. However, his outer blindness now gives him the clarity of his inner vision—his Ego is no longer in control but has the appropriate relation to the Self. As with Moses, the goals of Samson's Ego are subsumed to the higher goal that was ordained by God before his birth. He deals a great defeat to the Philistines—at least for the time being—dying in a heroic act that symbolically and literally brings the house of the Philistines down on them and himself:

> Then Samson said, "Let me die with the Philistines." He strained with all his might; and the house fell on the lords

---

53 Judges 16:17.

and all the people who were in it. So those he killed at his death were more than those he had killed during his life. Then his brothers and all his family came down and took him and brought him up and buried him between Zorah and Eshtaol in the tomb of his father Manoah. He had judged Israel for twenty years.[54]

Figure 7 The Blinded Samson

---

54 Judges 16:30–34.

Chapter 8

Saul: King and Prophet

> When Samuel became old, he made his sons judges over Israel. The name of his firstborn son was Joel, and the name of his second, Abijah; they were judges in Beersheba. Yet his sons did not follow in his ways, but turned aside after gain; they took bribes and perverted justice.
>
> Then all the elders of Israel gathered together and came to Samuel at Ramah, and said to him, "You are old and your sons do not follow in your ways; appoint for us, then, a king to govern us, like other nations." But the thing displeased Samuel when they said, "Give us a king to govern us."[55]

The story of Saul begins with the ruling principle in Israel—the prophet Samuel—being old, dissolute, and no longer able to rule effectively. Samuel has unwisely appointed his sons as judges over Israel. They follow the devices and desires of their Egos: "Yet his sons did not follow his ways, but turned aside after gain; they took bribes and perverted justice."[56] The leaders of Israel look to other nations for an answer to their problems and ask Samuel for a king to govern them, as other

---
55 I Samuel 8:1–5.
56 I Samuel 8:3.

nations had. Once again, they look outside themselves for someone to provide the solutions to their problems.

Samuel reports the people's demand for a king to God and receives some consolation for his bruised Ego. God tells him not to take it personally. "Just as they have done to me, from the day I brought them up out of Egypt to this day, forsaking me and serving other gods, so also they are doing to you."[57] He warns the people of the consequences of their demand—a long list that starts with taking their sons to chariots and ends with their enslavement. For people whose minds are made up and whose Egos are filled with desire, however, the die is cast—they will have a king like everyone else.

Helen Luke's analysis of Saul's kingship reveals a man who would be both king and prophet of Israel.[58] The account of Saul's anointing tells of Saul being sent to Gilgal by Samuel while Samuel prepares for the anointing. In the course of the journey, Saul meets a band of prophets and falls into a "prophetic frenzy" with them. Luke notes that a prophet was a seer or "one in whom the deep unconscious has been activated and to whom is given the choice between meeting and relating to the powers thus released or succumbing to possession by them."[59]

This attempt by Yahweh to give the Israelites what they demand is destined to fail. Luke notes that Yahweh appears to prematurely anticipate the union of opposites in one man who would be both king and prophet. At first, Saul's kingship seems successful. He defeats their

---

57 1 Samuel 8:8.
58 Helen M. Luke, *The Story of Saul, The Inner Story*, Crossroads, New York.
59 *The Inner Story*, 66.

perpetual nemeses, the Philistines—but in his success are the seeds of his downfall. Saul requires his troops to swear an oath that they will not eat until he has been avenged against his enemies, and they return home. His son Jonathan inadvertently breaks the oath, but Saul saves him from punishment. The Israelites initially experience continued success, defeating the Amalekites, but they disobey the command of God to utterly destroy all the people and all their possessions. At this, Samuel withdraws his counsel from Saul, and God is no longer with him. This rift is dramatically portrayed: "As Samuel turned to go away, Saul caught hold of the hem of his robe, and it tore. And Samuel said to him, 'The LORD has torn the kingdom of Israel from you this very day, and has given it to a neighbour of yours, who is better than you.'"[60] Samuel now anoints a new king to replace Saul: David.

Saul is torn between the demands and responsibilities that his kingship placed on him by his premature role. He identifies with the persona of king and lets that rule his action. His Ego is then the controlling factor that guides his life. He no longer follows the prophetic voice that had led to his selection as king. The voice of God in the person of Samuel is torn from him. As Luke declares, "He has chosen worldly power and betrayed the inner voice."[61]

Saul's story becomes ever more tragic as he hangs on to his persona of king, fighting the new order that is ordained by God. The story of his downfall is a true tragedy in every sense. Saul's Ego is well and truly defeated by his encounter with the Self—a defeat from which Saul never recovers. Throughout Saul's long, inevitable slide into oblivion, it can

---

60 I Samuel 15:27–28.
61 *The Inner Story*, 69.

be said that God has forsaken Saul, who no longer receives the visions and inspirations of a prophet. His role as king becomes less and less legitimate. A person in this state will become desperate to renew his relationship with the divine. We are told that when Saul faces the army of his nemeses, the Philistines, he becomes afraid. "When Saul inquired of the Lord, the Lord did not answer him, not by dreams, or by Urim or by prophets."[62] Saul in desperation consults a medium—the witch of Endor. He does this in violation of the prohibition against consulting witches. The spirit of Samuel, who is called forth, confirms that God has abandoned Saul and that Saul is doomed to die; Samuel proclaims, "Tomorrow you and your sons shall be with me."

Figure 8 Saul and the witch of Endor

---

62 1 Samuel 28:6.

Chapter 9

David: King and Visionary

> The LORD said to Samuel, "How long will you grieve over Saul? I have rejected him from being king over Israel. Fill your horn with oil and set out; I will send you to Jesse the Bethlehemite, for I have provided for myself a king among his sons."[63]

David is considered a hero, but not a classic one. We know nothing of his birth, so we have to assume there was nothing miraculous or marvellous about it. Also, there is no indication of him being twice born. There seems to be no predictor in his life to the greatness for which he is destined. However, given the wondrous deeds that David goes on to engage in, he must be considered a hero, and the founder of a line from which will come the long-awaited Messiah.

David first appears as a youth who is in the background of his family. He is the youngest child and therefore someone who would be destined for greatness in fairy tales—but not in history. There is no indication of the earth-changing events to follow for this youngest child. David is tending his family's sheep when Samuel comes to find the one who is intended to be the new king of Israel to replace Saul. After it becomes

---

63 I Samuel 16:1.

clear that none of the other brothers is intended to be the anointed, David is anointed by Samuel, and his journey to greatness begins.

The first indication of the greatness to come arrives early, as David's talent on the lyre brings him into contact with King Saul. Saul is uneasy, as his Ego is in a state of being overwhelmed by unconscious forces or "evil spirit from the Lord." God has departed from Saul. David's heroic qualities begin to show when he goes into service in the court of Saul, who loves him and makes him his armour bearer. David shines forth as a "golden child" who will bring new life to Israel. This promise has begun to be fulfilled, and his true hero status confirmed, as David challenges and then defeats the giant Goliath—the champion of the Israelites' nemeses, the Philistines. He does this clothed only in the armour of God, knowing that God will protect him, and armed only with the weapon of a shepherd—a sling. This audacious act is not a matter of Ego inflation. David is possessed by the archetype of the hero and so is able to carry out seemingly impossible things.

Figure 9 David Giving Thanks to God After the Death of Goliath

DAVID: KING AND VISIONARY

Evil continues to possess Saul, and jealousy and envy of David take over his life until a struggle for the kingdom ensues and Saul is killed in battle. The strife continues between Saul's family and David until David is finally victorious and the divided kingdom of Israel is united. Throughout his journey, David, possessed by the positive archetype of the hero, acts nobly, as shown in the two times he has Saul in his power and lets him live. This possession is shown most clearly when he is anointed as king over all Israel and peace reigns in the kingdom. The hero is united with the archetype of king: "David now becomes greater and greater, for the Lord, the God of hosts was with him."[64]

If this were a fairy tale, it might have ended here with "and they all lived happily ever after." However, a shadow is beginning to creep over the kingdom. We have a hint that the role or persona of king is now beginning to possess the Ego of David. He builds a fine house of cedar and takes many wives and concubines—acts befitting his station of king. David perceives that God has established him in his position and that Israel has been exalted through him. His Ego is now becoming identified with the role he has assumed, his Ego inflating and leading to a problematic relationship with the feminine in his psyche.

Another incident hints at his problem with the feminine, which will become significant for David in due course. He brings the Ark of the Covenant to his city so that God will reside with him in his capital city. As he enters the city, he is possessed by divine ecstasy, expressing the same by leaping and dancing in naked joy. His wife, Michal, the daughter of Saul, sees his demonstration, and she "despises him in her heart"

---

[64] 2 Samuel 5:10.

THE EGO AND THE BIBLE

and "had no child to the day of her death." No new life comes to David from this significant part of him—his last remaining connection to Saul, anointed by God as the first king of Israel.

The dissonance between David's Ego and his unconscious desires, which will bring David heartache, is not evident at this time. God makes a covenant with David in which He declares that David will be great and will have rest from his enemies. However, again there is an unsettling aspect that reveals things will not be entirely well. David reveals to God's representative, Nathan the prophet, his plan to build a home for the Ark of the Covenant—and therefore God—as he has built a home for himself. Prophets were people who had what could be considered a direct line to God. It was their calling to give God's word to the Jewish people. They often came into conflict with the rulers of their time when the people were not following God's plan for them. Nathan was a significant prophet in King David's rule.

At first, Nathan is in favour of this plan. However, God reveals that He has no desire for a house—or, at least, that David is not the one to build it. This instance shows the danger of believing that you know the mind of God, as your idea of His will often reflects your Ego's desires, rather than God's.

God declares that it will be David's son who will build the house. This poses the question: If David will do great things in the eyes of God, why did God not allow David to fulfil his plan in building a house for God? As we shall see, there is trouble ahead for David.

Trouble for David again takes the form of a beautiful woman. His desire to possess the feminine is manifest in the numerous wives and concubines he takes throughout his kingship. The first way in which this disrupted his outer life was his relationship with his wife Michal, Saul's daughter. This relationship became negative and produced no children—no new life in David's existence. His unconscious desire to possess the feminine takes hold of him, and he is overcome with desire for another outer form of his anima. From the roof of the house he had built for himself, he sees Bathsheba bathing on the roof of a neighbouring house. Filled with desire, he possesses her physically. When Bathsheba informs David of her pregnancy, he further exacerbates his crime with a scheme to cover up his liaison, having Bathsheba's husband, Uriah the Hittite, killed in battle. Bathsheba is sometimes depicted as a temptress to mitigate David's guilt. However, the biblical story shows that David is wholly at fault. The account begins with the time of the year being springtime when "kings go out to war." However, David, the great military leader, stays in Jerusalem as his army goes out to battle. When David sees Bathsheba, she is in the act of purifying herself after her period. While she follows this holiness code, David does not act in a manner suitable for the position he identifies with so strongly—the king. He allows the devices and desires of his Ego to rule him.

Nathan the prophet declares God's judgement on this evil act—or, rather, Nathan has David declare his own judgement through a parable of the rich man who takes a poor man's beloved lamb and slaughters it. This brings about David's repentance, but the judgement of God is that the child of the union will die—a case of the sins of the father falling on the child. Nathan declares that, because of his repentance, God will allow David to live. The child does die, as Nathan predicts—however, out of the union of David and Bathsheba will come David's successor, Solomon the wise.

More family troubles ensue, caused by David's relationship to the feminine being out of joint. These eventually lead to civil war between David and his son Absalom. First David's firstborn son, Amnon, rapes his half-sister, Tamar, being overwhelmed by desire for her. After he finally possesses her by stealth, he rejects her as spoiled goods, as she has now fallen off the pedestal on which he has placed her. The projection of his inner feminine that landed on her and which caused his desire is withdrawn and dies. This action is avenged by her brother Absalom, who eventually kills Amnon. David exiles Absalom, eventually leading to the civil war between father and son, as Absalom's ambition rules his actions.

The ambition of Absalom represents another example of the Ego's desire for honour, glory, and power leading to an ultimate downfall. Absalom is killed in the civil war between father and son. This tragedy has a great impact on David, who mourns the loss of his son deeply:

> The king was deeply moved, and went up to the chamber over the gate, and wept; and as he went, he said, "O my son Absalom, my son, my son Absalom! Would that I had died instead of you, O Absalom, my son, my son!"[65]

The experience of having lost his son under such terrible circumstances seems to have had a salutary effect on David. He shows mercy to Shimei, a supporter of Saul, who openly insulted and cursed him. This is the second time Shimei has cursed David and David has acted graciously to him. The first time, David appeared to be hedging his bets—thinking

---

65 2 Samuel 18:33.

that if he treated Shimei with kindness, God might reward him for tolerating the act. However, for this second act of mercy, his motives seem to be pure and his act a heartfelt one of kindness and mercy.

We leave David here on this high note, which is appropriate to one who accomplished much. Although he had a great struggle with the devices and desires of his Ego throughout his life, he always maintained a strong connection with his God. This is reflected in his last words:

> The spirit of the LORD speaks through me,
>
> his word is upon my tongue. The God of Israel has spoken,
>
> the Rock of Israel has said to me:
>
> One who rules over people justly,
>
> ruling in the fear of God, is like the light of morning,
>
> like the sun rising on a cloudless morning,
>
> gleaming from the rain on the grassy land.[66]

---

[66] 2 Samuel 23:2–4.

Chapter 10

Solomon the Wise

That night God appeared to Solomon, and said to him, "Ask what I should give you." Solomon said to God, "You have shown great and steadfast love to my father David, and have made me succeed him as king. O LORD God, let your promise to my father David now be fulfilled, for you have made me king over a people as numerous as the dust of the earth. Give me now wisdom and knowledge to go out and come in before this people, for who can rule this great people of yours?" God answered Solomon, "Because this was in your heart, and you have not asked for possessions, wealth, honour, or the life of those who hate you, and have not even asked for long life, but have asked for wisdom and knowledge for yourself that you may rule my people over whom I have made you king. Wisdom and knowledge are granted to you. I will also give you riches, possessions, and honor, such as none of the kings had who were before you, and none after you shall have the like."[67]

This is a propitious start to Solomon's reign. He seems to have been able to put away his Ego's desires upon ascending to the throne. He has what

---

[67] 2 Chronicles 1:7–12.

appears to be the ultimate opportunity to have his heart's or his Ego's desire. Yet he asks for wisdom to rule for the benefit of his people, rather than for any benefit for himself. Could anyone ask for a better start to the career of a leader? However, other leaders—after Solomon if not before—have started out with the best of intentions but have let power and prestige corrupt the purity of those intentions. Perhaps the very thing Solomon wished for—wisdom—would prevent this from happening.

David, his father, offers him sage advice at the end of his life:

> "I am about to go the way of all the earth. Be strong, be courageous, and keep the charge of the LORD your God, walking in his ways and keeping his statutes, his commandments, his ordinances, and his testimonies, as it is written in the law of Moses, so that you may prosper in all that you do and wherever you turn."[68]

The key to this advice is to keep walking in the ways of God and to keep his statues. Unless people have a strong relationship with the Self—the God Image in the psyche—they will need external rules to follow and aid them in doing the right thing in their lives. This is particularly true of someone in the position of power, such as Solomon, who is very much in danger of identifying with his persona of ruler and falling victim to an inflated Ego.

At first, things do go well with Solomon and the people of Israel. Under Solomon's rule, the country prospers as it never has before and has not since. It becomes a player on the world stage. Solomon builds, with God's permission, the first temple in Jerusalem. He draws material and

---

[68] 1 Kings 2:2–3.

THE EGO AND THE BIBLE

workmen from the corners of the world, and the result is one of the wonders of the world. Solomon rules with the wisdom granted to him by God, as shown by the famous account of the dispute of the two women who each claim the baby as their own. Solomon declares the child should be divided equally and each woman given a half. The true mother is revealed by her willingness to sacrifice her own interest to save the child. Solomon's fame as a wise and just ruler spreads far and wide, until the fabled Queen of Sheba visits him to see if what is said about him is true.

The visit of the Queen of Sheba seems to come to an excellent end, one that satisfies both Solomon and the queen. The two royal personages shower each other with gifts, and Solomon gives "the queen of Sheba every desire that she expressed."[69] One might infer that he did not mean only material goods.

Figure 10 Solomon and the Queen of Sheba

---

69 1 Kings 10:13.

Solomon's reign brings Israel fame and renown throughout the world. It seems that he has, using his gift of wisdom, become that rare thing—the ruler who ruled for the benefit of his dominion rather than for himself. Was Solomon then able to rule without his Ego at least trying to assert itself and become the overriding factor in his rule? We do find that he is not without flaw and his reign not without error. We find that Solomon's relationship with the feminine influences his Ego. The Bible states, "King Solomon loved many foreign women." This, it turns out, is a mastery of understatement, for we also read that "among his wives were seven hundred princesses and three hundred concubines; and his wives turned away his heart."[70] His Ego is ruled, at least in part, by the desire to possess the feminine in his psyche. In pursuing this desire, he breaks the commandment of God, as his father, David, had done. "For when Solomon was old, his wives turned away his heart after other gods; and his heart was not true to the LORD his God, as was the heart of his father David."[71]

Another indication that Solomon's reign was not without the shadow was revealed in the reign of his son, Rehoboam. Rehoboam, unfortunately, does not receive the gift of wisdom from God as his father had. He does not have the wisdom to take the wise counsel of the older men who had attended his father:

> Then King Rehoboam took counsel with the older men who had attended his father Solomon while he was still alive, saying, "How do you advise me to answer this

---
70 1 Kings 11:3.
71 1 Kings 11:4.

people?" They answered him, "If you will be kind to this people and please them, and speak good words to them, then they will be your servants for ever."[72]

Rather than heeding this wise counsel, he takes the counsel of the young men he had grown up with, who show the folly of youth:

> Thus should you speak to the people who said to you, "Your father made our yoke heavy, but you must lighten it for us"; tell them, "My little finger is thicker than my father's loins. Now, whereas my father laid on you a heavy yoke, I will add to your yoke. My father disciplined you with whips, but I will discipline you with scorpions."[73]

From this, we can conclude that those ruled by Solomon found his quest for fame and glory to be a heavy burden—one that would be even heavier under the rule of his son, who followed in his father's misplaced footsteps. We eventually see that, for all the blessings he received from God, Solomon's reign was very much an imperfect one, not immune from the devices and desires of the Ego.

---

[72] 2 Chronicles 10:6–7.
[73] 2 Chronicles 10:10–11.

Chapter 11

Esther the Queen

> In the second year of the reign of Ahasuerus the Great, on the first day of Nisan, Mordecai son of Jair son of Shimei son of Kish, of the tribe of Benjamin, had a dream…And this was his dream: Noises and confusion, thunders and earthquake, tumult on the earth! Then two great dragons came forward, both ready to fight, and they roared terribly. At their roaring every nation prepared for war, to fight against the righteous nation. It was a day of darkness and gloom, of tribulation and distress, affliction and great tumult on the earth! And the whole righteous nation was troubled; they feared the evils that threatened them, and were ready to perish. Then they cried out to God; and at their outcry, as though from a tiny spring, there came a great river, with abundant water; light came, and the sun rose, and the lowly were exalted and devoured those held in honour. Mordecai saw in this dream what God had determined to do, and after he awoke he had it on his mind, seeking all day to understand it in every detail.[74]

The story of Esther begins and ends with a dream, which is most appropriate when we are dealing with a component of the psyche such as

---
[74] Esther Addition A 11:1–2, 5–11.

THE EGO AND THE BIBLE

the Ego. Dreams are revelations of the energy that resides in the unconscious of an individual as well as the collective unconscious. In the Bible, and in some circles today, dreams are believed to come from God, or from—to look at it another way—the divine source of that unconscious energy, and of everything.

The story begins with a plot against the king of Persia, King Ahasuerus, or, as he is better known in history, Artaxerxes. Two eunuchs of the court plan to kill the king. This plan is discovered by Mordecai (Mardocheus, in Persian), a Jew who is subsequently rewarded by the king. We do not know the motive of these two plotters, but it is safe to conclude that it was probably an expression of the Ego-driven desire to gain power and control.

After this preamble, the story itself begins with trouble between King Ahasuerus and his queen, Vashti. The king holds a banquet for his officials. On the seventh day of the banquet (he apparently does things in a grand way), the king summons Queen Vashti to appear before everyone to show off her beauty. Queen Vashti refuses his royal command, with predictable consequences. He becomes enraged at her disobedience, and Vashti is permanently banished from his presence. This action is taken not only because of the affront to his pride but also because his officials fear Vashti's action would set a bad example to noble women in the kingdom, who might rebel against the king's officials.

While there is no stated motive for Vashti's rather reckless behaviour, we can surmise that she acts out of pride, which in this case—as in many—goes before the fall. Pride is a direct manifestation of the Ego becoming inflated and believing that the individual's position is unassailable.

ESTHER THE QUEEN

Vashti certainly seems to let her pride overwhelm her judgement and rule her. Likewise, Ahasuerus's behaviour is, we can surmise, a case of injured pride. We are told that, upon learning of Vashti's disobedience, "the king was enraged, and his anger burned within him."[75] This extreme emotion, as against a rational reaction, signals that he is possessed by a complex. In effect, we have a clash of two pride-filled Egos. However, there is also the court official who advises the king that it would be a disaster if the queen was not punished, and that chaos would ensue throughout the kingdom. The result is a kingdom-wide decree that "all women will give honour to their husbands, high and low alike."[76] As it was highly unlikely that an outbreak of radical feminism would occur in this time and place, this extreme reaction was based on a fear that the existing order was on a shaky foundation. The Ego, afraid of losing control, will go to great lengths to ensure that the status quo is maintained.

The scene is at this point set for our heroine, Esther, to become queen. Esther (Hadassah in Persian) is the cousin of Mordecai and one of the women chosen as candidates to replace Vashti as queen:

> Then the king's servants who attended him said, "Let beautiful young virgins be sought out for the king. And let the king appoint commissioners in all the provinces of his kingdom to gather all the beautiful young virgins to the harem in the citadel of Susa under the custody of Hegai, the king's eunuch, who is in charge of the women; let their cosmetic treatments be given them. And let the

---
75 Esther 1:12.
76 Esther 1:20.

girl who pleases the king be queen instead of Vashti." This pleased the king, and he did so.[77]

Figure 11 Queen Esther

Esther is eventually selected from all the candidates and crowned as queen. All appears well again, as order is restored to the kingdom. The king has a beautiful, and apparently obedient, queen, and all the women will maintain their proper places in kingdom.

However, in this peaceable kingdom, conflict soon arises. It takes the form of Haman, who has been appointed to the highest position in the court. All the king's servants are required to bow down and do obeisance to Haman. However, Mordecai, being an observant Jew, refuses

---
[77] Esther 2:2–4.

to do this. In reaction to this insult, Haman sets out to not only punish Mordecai but also destroy all the Jews in the kingdom. Haman's inflated Ego cannot tolerate any challenge to its position and therefore overreacts. Haman convinces King Ahasuerus to order the destruction of the Jews, based on the argument that the Jews follow their own laws and do not obey the king's laws. There is no indication that the Jews were fomenting trouble in the kingdom, so again we have a situation where the Ego cannot tolerate any possible challenge to its authority.

Mordecai learns of the plan and appeals to Esther to intercede with the king on behalf of her people, although the king has no knowledge that she is Jewish. Esther throws herself on the mercy of God to save His people and to give her the courage to appeal to the king. "O God, whose might is overall, hear the voice of the despairing, and save us from the hands of the evildoers. And save me from my fear."[78] Bolstered by the hope of God's protection, she presents her petition to the king, even with the threat of death hanging over her head, for death awaits those who presented themselves to the king in his inner court without being summoned. Unlike in the case of Queen Vashti, her predecessor, there is no question that Esther's Ego rules her actions. She is willing to sacrifice herself for the possibility of saving her people, even at the risk of her own life. In this Esther is able to overcome the instinct of her Ego for self-preservation and submit her Ego to a higher value, i.e., that of saving her people.

King Ahasuerus receives Esther with open arms and grants her petition. This is a striking contrast to his reaction to Vashti's behaviour. It does

---

[78] Esther 14:19.

not necessarily mean that King Ahasuerus has matured and is no longer Ego-bound, though; his reaction may have more to do with Esther's humble approach. However, it could also be evidence of God's intervention to soften the king's heart. Haman, unaware of the king's change of heart, plans to take personal revenge on Mordecai, and with his wife's encouragement, has a gallows fifty cubits high built for the execution. This is an example of the feminine failing Haman, as his wife—the outer expression of his inner feminine—encourages his inflation and leads him astray. For his treachery the fate of Haman is given in the following passage:

> Haman son of Hammedatha the Agagite, the enemy of all the Jews, had plotted against the Jews to destroy them, and had cast Pur—that is, "the lot"—to crush and destroy them; but when Esther came before the king, he gave orders in writing that the wicked plot that he had devised against the Jews should come upon his own head, and that he and his sons should be hanged on the gallows.[79]

It is fitting to end the story of Esther, heroine to the Jews, with the analysis of Mordecai's dream. This is a wonderful example of dream interpretation and is as applicable today as it was in these ancient days:

> And Mordecai said, "These things have come from God; for I remember the dream which I had concerning these matters, and none of them has failed to be fulfilled. There was the little spring that became a river,

---

[79] Esther 9: 24–25.

and there was light and sun and abundant water—the river is Esther, whom the king married, and made queen. The two dragons are Haman and myself. The nations are those that gathered to destroy the name of the Jews. And my nation, this is Israel, who cried out to God, and were saved. The Lord hath saved his people; the Lord has rescued us from all these evils; God has done great signs and great wonders, wonders that have never happened among the nations. For he made two lots, one for the people of God, and one for all the nations, and these two lots came to the hour and moment and day of decision before God among all the nations. And God remembered his people, and vindicated his inheritance. So they will observe these days in the month Adar, on the fourteenth and fifteenth day of the month, with an assembly and joy and gladness before God, from generation to generation forever among his people Israel."[80]

---

80 Esther 10:4–13.

Chapter 12

The Trials of Job

> There was once a man in the land of Uz whose name was Job. That man was blameless and upright, one who feared God and turned away from evil. There were born to him seven sons and three daughters. He had seven thousand sheep, three thousand camels, five hundred yoke of oxen, five hundred donkeys, and very many servants; so that this man was the greatest of all the people of the east. His sons used to go and hold feasts in one another's houses in turn; and they would send and invite their three sisters to eat and drink with them. And when the feast days had run their course, Job would send and sanctify them, and he would rise early in the morning and offer burnt-offerings according to the number of them all; for Job said, "It may be that my children have sinned, and cursed God in their hearts." This is what Job always did.[81]

Thus, the story of Job opens with an idyllic scene of a perfect life. Job is the best of men, living in the best of possible circumstances. He has a happy family. He is rich, by any measure. He has many servants and cattle. Above all, we are told he fears God and lives a blameless life—it is almost too good to be true.

---
81 Job 1:1–5.

THE TRIALS OF JOB

Reading this passage can leave us chilled, for we are certain such good fortune cannot last—conflict must arise. Otherwise, there would be little point in telling the story. As this account of a good man is included in Holy Scripture, we expect that God will enter the picture to save our hero from whatever evil befalls him, as in the case of Isaac, when he was about to be sacrificed by his father, Abraham. However, we discover that when evil does indeed enter to disrupt Job's idyllic life, it has an unexpected source.

Figure 12 The examination of Job, Satan pours on the plagues of Job

Job becomes a pawn in a celestial wager between God and Satan. Now, it must be understood that this was before Satan had been expelled from heaven after his revolt against God. He is one of the "heavenly beings" who come to present themselves before God. This situation, in effect, resembles a royal court of a king. Satan lives up to his name, which appropriately means "the accuser," and holds that Job's fear of God and blameless life mean nothing, as Job has never been put to the

THE EGO AND THE BIBLE

test. Satan bets God that if God will permit him to send troubles into Job's untroubled life, Job will curse God.

Satan does an exemplary job of troubling Job—killing his children and destroying his property—but still Job does not curse God. Satan ups the ante and, with God's permission, attacks Job's person, "inflicting loathsome sores on Job from the soles of his foot to the crown of his head"; yet Job's faith in God holds firm. Job is further afflicted, however; rather than Satan, so-called friends visit him this time, insisting that Job's troubles must be due to Job's own actions. Job demands an opportunity to appear before God to seek justice. God permits this but then attacks Job's impertinence in questioning God's actions, as a mere human is not in a position to question the creator of the universe. Job wisely defers to God's omnipotence, and his fortunes are restored and even increased. He is blessed with new possessions and children. As a bonus, Job's erstwhile friends are punished.

This story has a small cast of characters—principally Job, Satan, and God, with minor roles for Job's friends and family members. What role do the Egos of these characters play in the drama of Job's story? Edward Edinger has identified a Job archetype.

Archetypes are "forms of psychic energy which are innate, universal prototypes for ideas and may be used to interpret observations." They are the natural forces residing in the collective unconscious, as identified by Jung, which underlie all human life throughout human history, independent of personal experience. Edinger outlines the features of this archetype. He notes many examples in sacred history, e.g., Jacob wrestling with the angel, Arjuna and Krishna, Paul and Christ, Moses

THE TRIALS OF JOB

and El-Khidr, and Jung and Philemon.[82] The chief features of the Job archetype are:

1. An encounter between the Ego and the Greater Personality (God, supreme being, angels)

2. A wound or suffering of the Ego as a result of the encounter

3. The perseverance of the Ego, which endures the ordeal and persists in scrutinizing the experience in search of its meaning

4. A divine revelation by which the Ego is rewarded with some insight into the transpersonal psyche.[83]

Here we see the role that the Ego plays with our protagonist, Job. However, let us take a closer look at Job's Ego at the beginning of this adventure, when he encounters God, or the transpersonal psyche, in Edinger's term. Job is presented as someone who does not seem to have any problem with Ego inflation. He is secure in his position, fears God, and lives a blameless and upright life. However, at the end of the opening description, there is a hint that perhaps Job is not all that balanced in his perspective of himself.

Job makes a burnt offering to God. "For Job says, 'It may be that my children have sinned, and cursed God in their hearts.'"[84] There is no hint

---
82 *Encounter with the Self*, 11.
83 Ibid.
84 Job 1:5.

that Job has any doubt that he might be one who sins. His certainty that he is not guilty of any significant sin could indicate that he has a significant shadow—that part of the personality unrecognized or denied by the Ego. He reminds me somewhat of the Pharisee in Jesus's parable, the one who gives thanks to God that he is unlike the tax collector praying next to him.[85] Although Job does not voice his belief in his superiority, he could easily fall into that perfection complex. The Pharisee does everything that the law commands, and his very consciousness of that fact leads to the sin of pride. Job also lives a life that is apparently in full compliance with God's laws.

However, Job does seem to possess great Ego strength. His Ego is able to persevere in the face of attacks by the accuser. His friends and even God, show him no mercy in all that God allows Satan to put him through. In the end of the encounter with God, Job receives insight into the personality of God. We must consider God in terms of the personal in our consideration of the role of the Ego. In one of Jung's more controversial propositions, *Answer to Job*—his exposition of the book of Job—he proposes that the God of the Old Testament, Yahweh, is an amoral being, acting primarily out of instinct. "Yahweh is a phenomenon and as Job says, 'not a man.'"[86] God is not moral or immoral but amoral, for as Jung notes, "Morality presupposes consciousness."[87] Jung notes that Yahweh is unconscious, having an animal nature in Ezekiel's vision, which "attributes three-fourths animal nature and only one-fourth human nature"[88] to the deity. It is God's unconscious

---
85 Luke 18:9–14.
86 *Answer to Job* in *The Portable Jung*, 547.
87 *Answer to Job*, 547.
88 Ibid.

THE TRIALS OF JOB

nature that Job encounters with such serious consequences. Jung proposes that God's—from our perspective—immoral behaviour toward Job is due to the possibility that "a suspicion [has] grown up in God that man possesses an infinitely small yet more concentrated light than he, Yahweh possesses? A jealousy of that kind might perhaps explain his behaviour."[89] In effect, God is jealous of Job's consciousness and consequently of his Ego.

Satan is another divine creature we would not normally consider as having an Ego. However, Satan, traditionally thought of as one of God's chief angels, is presented in the Book of Job as someone who is very much in possession of an Ego. Satan is a descendent of the serpent—the character we encountered in the creation story, whom God placed in the Garden of Eden and who tempted the first humans. Satan is often depicted as serpent or dragon in apocalyptic literature, so we can see Satan as a close relative of the character in Genesis who was condemned to go upon his belly and to eat the dust; he was denied the arms and legs he had originally, at his creation, been granted by God.

In the book of Job, Satan is now tempting God, rather than the first humans. He tempts God to prove that His most worthy subject will remain faithful to Him despite tragedy entering his life. Satan reveals his pride in believing he can defeat God in a contest. God appears to behave toward Satan as a permissive parent; Satan suffers no consequences for his underhanded behaviour—at least at this point. Perhaps if God had been harder on Satan at this point, events would not have gotten out of hand later. This pride develops until it inevitably leads to his fall from

---

[89] *Answer to Job*, 538.

THE EGO AND THE BIBLE

heaven to earth, as noted by Jesus.[90] He shows the definite symptoms of a seriously inflated Ego, which will lead to serious but necessary consequences for him, and for all of humankind.

The story of Job is a comedy in the literary sense, with all restored as it should be at the end of the events. Job was is rewarded for the perseverance of his Ego. He is rewarded not just by his possessions and new family but by his insight into the nature of the divine.

---

90 Luke 10:18.

Chapter 13

Jonah: Encountering God in the Belly of the Beast

> Now the word of the LORD came to Jonah son of Amittai, saying, "Go at once to Nineveh, that great city, and cry out against it; for their wickedness has come up before me." But Jonah set out to flee to Tarshish from the presence of the LORD. He went down to Joppa and found a ship going to Tarshish; so he paid his fare and went on board, to go with them to Tarshish, away from the presence of the LORD.

Jonah's reaction to his encounter with God is to run away in the opposite direction as fast as he can. This could be considered a defeat for the Ego; however, it seems that it was more a matter of his survival instinct kicking in in a very strong way. Jonah did not have a true encounter with the divine—at least not initially. Jonah's Ego seems to have survived the encounter intact and still in charge. He decides to get as far away from God, and the destiny that God has arranged for him, as possible.

From his Ego's point of view, this is a very reasonable thing to do. What God instructed him to do would be the equivalent of walking down Wall Street in New York, telling the financial gurus and manipulators to repent before God destroyed them. Nineveh was the equivalent of

THE EGO AND THE BIBLE

New York in its heyday—the most powerful city-state in the world. Of course, if a modern-day Jonah was to walk down Wall Street carrying a sign saying "repent" and shouting that the end is near, he would likely end up in a mental hospital. In Nineveh, however, he more likely would meet a quick and certain end at the hand of the troops of the king; this is why Jonah believed that God was sending him on a suicide mission. He very reasonably desired to avoid this fate.

We do not know anything about Jonah prior to this encounter with the divine. However, it appears that this may have been the first experience for him. It seems he is completely unprepared for his encounter with the Self. He does not accept the mission impossible that God has designated for him, unlike other people whose stories are recorded in the Bible. Abram willingly picked up all his possessions and went to an unknown country at God's decree, without giving it a second thought, according to the records. "Now the LORD said to Abram, 'Go from your country and your kindred and your father's house to the land that I will show you.'"[91] Moses was more reluctant than that man later named Abraham by God. However, after some discussion with the voice in the burning bush, he consented to do as God had commanded. Jonah definitely believes that he can disagree with God and run to a hiding place where God will not find him. However, he discovers there is no hiding place from God.

Jonah boards a ship to go to Tarshish, away from the presence of the Lord. A storm arises—presumably of divine origin—and it seems that Jonah accepts that his fate is inevitable, as he confesses that he is the cause of the tempest. Jonah faces up to his responsibility, and, to save

---

91 Genesis 12:1.

themselves, the crew eventually throws Jonah to swim with the fishes. Here, Jonah shows a maturity of Ego strength that he did not have before. He faces the consequences of his attempt to avoid the fate God has prepared for him and saves his fellow travellers.

Figure 13 Jonah Cast Forth by the Whale.

Jonah now spends the requisite three days and three nights in the belly of the great fish (contrary to popular belief, it is not a whale). During this time of preparation and incubation, Jonah faces his dark night of the soul. He is now ready to accept God's plan and is resurrected from the depths. Jonah has encountered the Self, and it remains to be seen, at this point, if his Ego will simply be defeated temporarily or if he is genuinely to be transformed by the experience.

Jonah does as God commands and declares God's judgement on the great city of Nineveh. Surprise, surprise and miracle of miracles—the king and all the city heed Jonah's warning and repent, covering every living thing—man, woman, child, and even their animals—in sackcloth and ashes. Heeding their cries of repentance, God changes His mind, and the city is saved. Contrary to what we might expect, Jonah does not rejoice that his warning has been heeded and that his efforts have produced bountiful fruit. He becomes angry that God has changed His mind and not followed through with His plan to destroy Nineveh and all its inhabitants. Jonah believes that God should behave as Jonah wants Him to. Jonah believes that he knows better than God what should happen. We see at this point that his Ego has not yet been transformed by his encounter with God in the belly of the great fish.

Jonah now goes out and sulks under a tree, waiting to see what will happen to Nineveh and likely hoping that God will change His mind back and destroy it. God makes a bush grow over Jonah to comfort him, which gives Jonah happiness. God then sends a worm to attack and kill the bush. The hot sun and sultry wind now make Jonah so miserable that he declares it would be better to die than to live this way. God then gives Jonah his final lesson:

> But God said to Jonah, "Is it right for you to be angry about the bush?" And he said, "Yes, angry enough to die." Then the LORD said, "You are concerned about the bush, for which you did not labour and which you did not grow; it came into being in a night and perished in a night. And should I not be concerned about Nineveh, that great city, in which there are more than a hundred

and twenty thousand people who do not know their right hand from their left, and also many animals?"[92]

The story of Jonah ends here, but we hope that he has finally been transformed by this final encounter with the divine.

---

92 Jonah 4:9–11.

Chapter 14

Jeremiah: Receiver of the Word

> Now the word of the LORD came to me saying,
>
> "Before I formed you in the womb I knew you,
>
> and before you were born I consecrated you;
>
> I appointed you a prophet to the nations."[93]

Jeremiah experiences what is common to prophets and seers—a breaking through into the consciousness of the divine energy from the collective unconscious, which is the source of all religious experience. Jung describes the significance of this part of the psyche:

> The collective unconscious—so far as we can say anything about it at all—appears to consist of mythological motifs or primordial images, for which reason the myths of all nations are its real exponents. In fact, the whole of mythology could be taken as a sort of projection of the collective unconscious…We can therefore study the collective unconscious in two ways, either in mythology or in the analysis of the individual.[94]

---

93 Jeremiah 1:4–5.
94 *The Structure of the Psyche*, CW 8, par. 325.

JEREMIAH: RECEIVER OF THE WORD

Jeremiah has a reaction similar to others in his situation, both before and after him—he doubts his ability to fulfil the assignment given to him by God. "Then I said, 'Ah, Lord GOD! Truly I do not know how to speak, for I am only a boy.'"[95] However, as we know, God does not give up that easily. God reaffirms that Jeremiah is the one to undertake the momentous task and that he could refuse, but at his peril. "But you, gird up your loins; stand up and tell them everything that I command you. Do not break down before them, or I will break you before them."[96] Jeremiah is commanded to tell the people that God is going to punish them for their unfaithfulness. Jeremiah has encountered the divine, and his Ego is now identified with the Self. He is now the tool by which God's word will be delivered to the people. His condition is dramatically described by Megan McKenna:

> From the first words of Yahweh's call to Jeremiah, we know we are in the presence of a passionate man, torn and broken by what he must say and what he will witness among his beloved people. His relationship with his God is braided together with his relationship with his people, and both are sources of grief, agony, tears, and on rare occasions, joy and delight.[97]

---

95 Jeremiah 1:6.
96 Jeremiah 1:17.
97 *Prophets, Words of Fire*, 104.

Figure 14 The Prophet Jeremiah

As with Nineveh, God gives Israel an opportunity to repent and return to Him. However, as McKenna notes, at this point Israel is, "a nation without honour, without justice, without any tenderness in its soul for the poor and needy, for the fatherless, the widow, and the orphan."[98] Israel is suffering from a collective state of Ego inflation. Israel's collective consciousness, in other words, believes that it no longer needs to follow the God of Abraham, Isaac, and Moses.

Jeremiah is caught between two extremes. On one hand, he is identified with God, who is demanding justice for the unfaithfulness of Israel yet desires to deliver mercy to His people if they will repent. On the other hand, he identifies with his people and is overcome with sorrow for what he sees as the consequences for the apostasy of Israel. He is, in

---

98 Ibid., 106.

effect, torn apart by these extremes and what Friedrich von Hügel calls the divinely intended tension of his call. As McKenna describes,

> Jeremiah is shunted back and forth between extremes. He knows in his flesh and mind that God's words are "like fire, like the hammer that shatters a rock" (Jer. 23:29). Because Yahweh's continual call to repentance has been ignored, it becomes a judgement handed down: "All land will be a ruin and a desolation and for seventy years these nations will serve the king of Babylon" (Jer. 25:11). Jeremiah knows that this word of Yahweh is directed not only to Judah and Jerusalem but also to all the nations of the earth.[99]

To a great extent, Jeremiah is subsumed in the divine. His Ego is now identified with the persona and role of the prophet, who is the voice of God, delivering God's message to God's people—who are also Jeremiah's people. Jeremiah is so identified with the role that he becomes the archetype of the prophet and is identified as the consummate prophet, who will speak truth to power regardless of the consequences. As McKenna notes, there are consequences:

> He suffers what will become the earmark of the true prophet: persecution, humiliation, plots against him, and attempts to murder him. Jehoiakim, the son of King Josiah, arrests him and has him sentenced to death… Jeremiah continues to do battle with the kings of Judah

---

[99] Ibid., 111.

THE EGO AND THE BIBLE

and the court prophets as Nebuchadnezzar's army draws closer.[100]

This fate is possible for anyone whose Ego is assimilated to the Self. He or she will live a life that is at odds with the collective consciousness of the culture. It is not a journey to be undertaken lightly.

Jeremiah follows his divine purpose and ends by going into exile into Babylon, with his people. In captivity, Jeremiah continues his prophetic call and does not hesitate to prophesy the disaster that would ultimately befall Babylon. We will end this journey of Jeremiah's with his prophecy:

> Jeremiah wrote in a scroll all the disasters that would come on Babylon, all these words that are written concerning Babylon. And Jeremiah said to Seraiah: "When you come to Babylon, see that you read all these words, and say, 'O LORD, you yourself threatened to destroy this place so that neither human beings nor animals shall live in it, and it shall be desolate for ever.' When you finish reading this scroll, tie a stone to it, and throw it into the middle of the Euphrates, and say, 'Thus shall Babylon sink, to rise no more, because of the disasters that I am bringing on her.'" Thus far are the words of Jeremiah.[101]

---

100 Ibid., 111.
101 Jeremiah 51:60–64.

Chapter 15

Huldah the Prophetess

As with women generally in history, women prophets or prophetesses are often in the background of biblical stories. The Bible, as with history, is often written by the victors and the ones who are in positions of power. However, a few prophetesses of note made it into the canon of Holy Scripture. Huldah, who was a contemporary of Jeremiah, had a small but telling role in the story of God's chosen people. Huldah's story begins with Josiah ascending to the kingship of Judah at the tender age of eight. Despite his youth, he becomes a righteous ruler. This is after a long line of kings who led the people away from the worship of the true God and encouraged the people to follow false gods.

Josiah attempts to bring in reforms that would correct the people's idolatry and sets about to restore the temple to its former glory. During the renovations, the book of Laws (and possibly the book of Deuteronomy) is discovered. This discovery is timely, as Judah has almost completely abandoned the law handed down to Moses by Yahweh. The book of Laws sets out the punishment that will befall the people due to their idolatry. Officials, including the high priest, Hilkiah, bring word of the discovery to King Josiah, who laments the judgement found in this book. In his wisdom, Josiah commands Hilkiah:

> "Go, inquire of the LORD for me, for the people, and for all Judah, concerning the words of this book that has been found; for great is the wrath of the LORD that is kindled against us, because our ancestors did not obey the words of this book, to do according to all that is written concerning us."[102]

It is telling that the high priest goes to the prophet Huldah to "inquire of the Lord." The action by the high priest in seeking the words of God from a woman prophet is unusual behaviour for the time. Prophets were normally men, and a woman, even one who might be in the role of prophet, would not have been consulted for major issues. However, perhaps it is a sign that the high priest knows radical action is required for the collective consciousness of the people to be called back to the true divine source of their being. The female personification of energy in the psyche—the anima—is a guide for the soul to the divine centre, the Self.

Huldah declares to them:

> "Thus says the Lord, the God of Israel: 'Tell the man who sent you to me, Thus says the Lord, I will indeed bring disaster on this place and on its inhabitants—all the words of the book that the king of Judah has read.'"[103]

Huldah has a certain similarity to Jeremiah in that she speaks God's truth and treats all the officials, from the high priest to the king, without

---
102 2 Kings 22:13.
103 2 Kings 22:15–16.

ceremony. God's words, which Huldah transmits to them, are straightforward and without ceremony: "tell that man who sent you." However, the king is more willing to listen to the Word of the Lord at this point and brings in reforms:

> The king went up to the house of the LORD, and with him went all the people of Judah, all the inhabitants of Jerusalem, the priests, the prophets, and all the people, both small and great; he read in their hearing all the words of the book of the covenant that had been found in the house of the LORD. The king stood by the pillar and made a covenant before the LORD, to follow the LORD, keeping his commandments, his decrees, and his statutes, with all his heart and all his soul, to perform the words of this covenant that were written in this book. All the people joined in the covenant.[104]

Despite the reforms, judgement does fall upon Judah as Huldah predicts. However, Josiah does not die in peace, contrary to her prediction. We see from Huldah's story that women are just as able as men to be identified with the Self and to become conduits for the divine Word.

---

[104] 2 Kings 23:2–3.

Chapter 16

Daniel: Tamer of Lions and Interpreter of Dreams

This story begins, as often is the case, with trouble for God's people. Judah has been besieged and captured by King Nebuchadnezzar of Babylon. The Babylonian captivity has begun. However, there is no talk of Israel's transgressions against God causing these troubles. Rather, we are introduced to Daniel and his three companions, Shadrach, Meshach, and Abednego, who are chosen to be part of the king's court. These were exemplary examples of young Israelite manhood, "without physical defect and handsome, versed in every branch of wisdom, endowed with knowledge and insight, and competent to serve in the king's palace."[105]

Daniel, the leader of the young men, shows wisdom beyond his years and, despite the temptations of the court, "resolves that he will not defile himself with the royal rations of food and wine."[106] It is not clear from the text why this would defile Daniel and his companions. That said, they show maturity beyond their years and stay true to their beliefs, consuming only vegetables and water. This causes consternation for the guard appointed to them, as he fears the consequences if they

---
[105] 1 Daniel 4.
[106] Daniel 1:8.

DANIEL: TAMER OF LIONS AND INTERPRETER OF DREAMS

suffer under this vegetarian (if not vegan) diet. However, Daniel again shows his maturity by proposing what might be one of the earliest scientific tests. The progress of Daniel and his companions is compared to other young men who partake of the royal rations. Surprisingly, after a short trial of ten days, the Israelites "appeared better and fatter than all the young men."

This raises an interesting possibility for our exploration of the Ego. Did Daniel and his companions have sufficient Ego strength to maintain their faith in the face of the possible consequences from their capture, and in the face of obvious temptations for young men—such as the delight of the royal rations—or were their Egos completely subsumed by the tenets of their religion, so that they did not have the Ego strength to try other possibilities in their lives? Their Egos could have succumbed to the dangers of inflation, since they were chosen as such exemplary examples of Israelite young manhood by their captors. However, by all indications, these temptations do not go to their heads; all four appear to have a strong religious faith and to maintain correctness in their actions. They appear to have a good balance of Ego strength and religious faith.

This episode gives only hints of the exceptional nature of these four golden young men. We are told that when they are examined by the king, "In every matter of wisdom and understanding concerning which the king inquired of them, he found them ten times better than all the magicians and enchanters in his whole kingdom. And Daniel continued there until the first year of King Cyrus."[107]

---

107 Daniel 1:12–20.

THE EGO AND THE BIBLE

This portentous beginning leads to even better things for Daniel and his companions. King Nebuchadnezzar is troubled by a dream. He is, however, every analyst's nightmare. He demands that the magicians, enchanters, and sorcerers not only interpret his dream but know the content of his dream without him having told them—all this on the pain of being torn limb from limb. This is not just a royal whim; he shows his wisdom in this demand, as he believes that if these early dream analysts can actually tell him the content of the dream, he will be able to trust their interpretation. The court wise men tell him, quite sensibly, that no one on earth can do such a thing. However, as king, Nebuchadnezzar does not need to act sensibly, and he decrees that all wise men of Babylon be executed. This includes Daniel and his companions, and they are commanded to appear before the king. All four men then appeal to God, and Daniel blesses God, who makes both the dream and its meaning manifest.

Daniel appears before the king and, giving God the credit, offers the dream and its interpretation. We have here confirmation that Daniel is in a transforming relationship with the Self. His Ego, subsumed, is not trying to maintain its position as the centre of the psyche. The dream that the king dreams is of a great statue with a head of gold, chest and arms of silver, middle and thighs of bronze, legs of iron, and feet partly of iron and partly of clay. A stone struck the feet of the statue, and it broke into pieces that blow away as chaff in the wind.

The dream interpretation reveals that in the dream, the symbol of the head of gold represented King Nebuchadnezzar. After King Nebuchadnezzar, there will arise inferior kingdoms—those of silver and bronze and, finally, two kingdoms—of iron and clay—that will be joined together, partly strong and partly weak. The stone that crushed the kingdoms will come from the hand of God, who will set up a kingdom that shall never be destroyed. The king is duly impressed and honours him. Daniel and his companions are rewarded with gifts. Daniel is made ruler over the province of Babylon and appoints his companions to government positions.

However, unlike in fairy tales, there is seldom a happily ever after in biblical stories. The king does not benefit from the divine wisdom revealed in the dream. King Nebuchadnezzar takes the dream literally rather than symbolically and focusses on the image in the dream, believing he can make it concrete. He makes a statue like the one in the dream; the real one is sixty cubits; approximately one hundred feet high. The king is so enthralled with this image from his unconscious that he sets it up as an object of worship. In effect, he sees the image itself as divine, rather than as a way to the divine. He then requires that all subjects bow down and worship it. The Chaldeans—the official dream interpreters whom the king has placed under Daniel's authority—report to the king that Shadrach, Meshach, and Abednego are not obeying the king's decree to worship the statue. We can see the green-eyed monsters of envy and pride raising their heads. The Chaldeans are, of course, envious of Daniel—a foreigner and a mere amateur—being placed over them; this act would have understandably hurt their pride. They would have welcomed an opportunity to seek revenge against the companions of Daniel. Their hurt Egos would then have been salved, and revenge would have been a dish served cold.

In reality, though, it will be a hot experience, rather than a cold one, for the three. They refuse to bow down to an idol. They remain faithful to God and follow the commandment not to have any other god. As a result, they are sentenced to be thrown into the now-famous fiery furnace. They are not singed by the flames, though, but are seen walking around, singing hymns of praise and praying to God. Their prayer—much longer than we are used to—begins, "Blessed are you, O Lord, God of our ancestors, and worthy of praise, and glorious is your name forever."[108] After many verses in which they recite the sins of the people and offer supplications, it ends, "Let them know that you alone are the Lord God, glorious over the whole world."[109] God responds and does just that. The servants attending to the fire stoke it with naphtha, pitch, tow, and brushwood—but to no avail, for:

> the angel of the Lord came down into the furnace to be with Azariah and his companions, and drove the fiery flames out of the furnace and made the inside of the furnace as though a moist wind were whistling through it.[110]

The three in the furnace respond to this epiphany with one voice of praise, glorifying God. King Nebuchadnezzar and all his officials then see that the fire had no power over the three—not a hair on their heads was singed. And he says, "Blessed be the God of Shadrach, Meshach, and Abednego, who has sent his angel and delivered his servants who trusted in him."[111] The king once again responds by promoting the three to high positions in Babylon.

---

108 Daniel 3:26.
109 Daniel 3:45.
110 Daniel 3:49.
111 Daniel 3:95.

DANIEL: TAMER OF LIONS AND INTERPRETER OF DREAMS

All is well, and King Nebuchadnezzar is "living at ease" in his house when he has a second dream that greatly disturbs him. Once again, he calls all the "magicians, the enchanters, the Chaldeans, and the diviners" to give him an interpretation, but none is able to provide one. At last, Daniel arrives and this time, he is told the dream. The dream is of a tree at the centre of the earth, which sheltered all the animals in its shade. A holy watcher comes from heaven and declares that the tree should be cut down and "he" should be with the animals until seven times have passed.

Daniel provides an interpretation that would fit very well with how dreams may be interpreted today. The dream is exceptional, as it declares that the tree is actually the dreamer. The dream predicts that if the dreamer continues his present course, he will lose his rational thought and be as an animal. In effect, he is heading for a mental breakdown—probably a psychotic break. Daniel provides an interpretation that is fitting for the context of King Nebuchadnezzar:

> Then Daniel, who was called Belteshazzar, was severely distressed for a while. His thoughts terrified him. The king said, "Belteshazzar, do not let the dream or the interpretation terrify you." Belteshazzar answered, "My lord, may the dream be for those who hate you, and its interpretation for your enemies! The tree that you saw, which grew great and strong, so that its top reached to heaven and was visible to the end of the whole earth, whose foliage was beautiful and its fruit abundant, and which provided food for all, under which animals of the

field lived, and in whose branches the birds of the air had nests—it is you, O king! You have grown great and strong. Your greatness has increased and reaches to heaven, and your sovereignty to the ends of the earth. And whereas the king saw a holy watcher coming down from heaven and saying, 'Cut down the tree and destroy it, but leave its stump and roots in the ground, with a band of iron and bronze, in the grass of the field; and let him be bathed with the dew of heaven, and let his lot be with the animals of the field, until seven times pass over him'—this is the interpretation, O king, and it is a decree of the Most High that has come upon my lord the king: You shall be driven away from human society, and your dwelling shall be with the wild animals. You shall be made to eat grass like oxen, you shall be bathed with the dew of heaven, and seven times shall pass over you, until you have learned that the Most High has sovereignty over the kingdom of mortals, and gives it to whom he will. As it was commanded to leave the stump and roots of the tree, your kingdom shall be re-established for you from the time that you learn that Heaven is sovereign. Therefore, O king, may my counsel be acceptable to you: atone for your sins with righteousness, and your iniquities with mercy to the oppressed, so that your prosperity may be prolonged.'"

Nothing the dream foretells happens for twelve months. You can imagine that the king begins breathing easily again, thinking the prediction of the dream will not come true this time. However, the king is walking on the roof of his royal palace. He believes he is literally the king of all he surveys. He declares, "Is this not magnificent Babylon, which I have built as a royal capital by my mighty power and for my glorious majesty?"[112] Immediately, a voice from heaven declares that the dream will be fulfilled, and the king becomes as an animal; he is driven away from human society, and he eats grass as an ox until the declared period of time has passed. Once he has recovered from this ordeal, the king wisely gives honour to God, "the King of heaven." In this case, the Ego becomes completely identified with the persona of the person. King Nebuchadnezzar is nothing but the king of Babylon. That leads to inflation that has nowhere to go but down from the great height to which it had soared.

The story shifts and a new king is on the throne. King Belshazzar holds a great feast for the lords of Babylon. While he is "under the influence of the wine," he commands that all the holy vessels from the temple in Jerusalem be brought out, and all those attending the banquet use them in their celebration. Immediately, the divine breaks through, and a finger begins to write on the plaster of the wall. In terror, he calls all the wise men and Chaldeans and the diviners to interpret the writing. However, he appears not to be aware of the ability of Daniel as interpreter of King Nebuchadnezzar's dreams. However, the queen, who is aware of Daniel, informs the king of his ability to interpret divine messages. The Ego of King Belshazzar holds sway as it once had for Nebuchadnezzar, and the spirit of the wine allows negative forces to enter into his consciousness. The divine has broken through his

---

112 Daniel 4:30.

conscious and overwhelmed his Ego. It is interesting that it is the feminine presence that informs the king of Daniel and his ability. The queen, who can be considered a personification of the anima—the feminine in his psyche—is the one who brings him into relationship with what is the archetype of the wise old man.

Daniel is called and interprets the inscription:

> mene, mene, tekel, and parsin. "This is the interpretation of the matter: mene, God has numbered the days of your kingdom and brought it to an end; tekel, you have been weighed on the scales and found wanting; peres, your kingdom is divided and given to the Medes and Persians."[113]

As with King Nebuchadnezzar, King Belshazzar rewards Daniel. However, that night, the prediction in the dream is realized. King Belshazzar dies and Darius, the Mede, receives the great kingdom of Babylon.

Daniel distinguishes himself in the service of King Darius and is appointed to a high position. Soon he distinguishes himself above all others, and Darius proposes to appoint him above all others. This prospect stirs up the envy and resentment of the other officials, who devise a plot against him. They realize that, as Daniel is without flaw, they can only trap him with his faithfulness to God's law. The conspirators propose to Darius that anyone who worships anything other than Darius for thirty days be thrown into a den of lions. Darius agrees and orders this to be.

---

113 Daniel 5:25–28.

DANIEL: TAMER OF LIONS AND INTERPRETER OF DREAMS

Figure 15 Daniel's Answer to the King

Despite the proclamation, Daniel continues praying to God three times a day. The conspirators are aware of Daniel's practice and report him to the king. Although it distresses Darius, he has no option but to follow his own decree and has Daniel thrown to the lions. Daniel is saved from the lions, however, as Shadrach, Meshach, and Abednego were saved from the fiery furnace. The next morning, to his great relief, King Darius finds Daniel safe and sound. As the king reports, God sent an angel to shut the lions' mouths. The king responds to this divine intervention:

> I make a decree, that in all my royal dominion people should tremble and fear before the God of Daniel:
> For he is the living God,
> enduring for ever.

His kingdom shall never be destroyed,
and his dominion has no end. He delivers and rescues,
he works signs and wonders in heaven and on earth;
for he has saved Daniel
from the power of the lions.[114]

---

114 Daniel 6:26–27.

Chapter 17

Jesus of Nazareth: Christ and Messiah

I believe in God,
the Father almighty,
creator of heaven and earth.
I believe in Jesus Christ, his only Son, our Lord.
He was conceived by the power of the Holy Spirit
and born of the Virgin Mary.
He suffered under Pontius Pilate,
was crucified, died, and was buried.
He descended to the dead.
On the third day he rose again.
He ascended into heaven,
and is seated at the right hand of the Father.
He will come again
to judge the living and the dead.
I believe in the Holy Spirit,
the holy catholic Church,
the communion of saints,

> the forgiveness of sins,
> the resurrection of the body,
> and the life everlasting.[115]

For Christians, the story of Jesus Christ is the pivotal point in the story of God's people. Jesus is revealed as the second person in the Trinity—the only begotten son of God the Father. As such, he is greater than the demigods so prevalent in the myths of other religions in Roman, Greek, and Oriental lands at that time. He was more than the product of the forced mating between a god such a Zeus, in the form of a swan, and a human such as Leda. The offspring of such a union had attributes of a god, such as superhuman strength. However, the offspring did not have attributes that made him an actual god, such as immortality. Hercules, the last mortal son of Zeus, was an exception, as he, according to the myth, became a god on his death. However, there was no immortality for other human offspring of gods.

In the case of Jesus, God did not take the form of swan, but rather impregnated Mary (whether she consented is ambiguous in the account) by the Holy Spirit—the third person of the Christian Trinity of God in three persons. Jesus, unlike the demigods, is held to be fully human and fully divine. He is of one substance with the Father, as it states in the Apostles' Creed of the Christian religion, as shown above. The question arising from this state of Jesus of Nazareth is: Does Jesus have an Ego, as other conscious humans do, and if so, how is that Ego manifest?

Scripture contains stories of Jesus's miraculous conception and birth. As noted in the creed, his mother, Mary, was a virgin who conceived

---

115 Apostles' Creed

Jesus through the power of the Holy Spirit. His birth—unlike that of many gods and demigods—was in lowly estate. He is born in a stable in an insignificant town, Bethlehem, in the unimportant country of Judea. His mother, Mary, and stepfather, Joseph, are humble, insignificant people. Joseph is a carpenter who takes pity on his betrothed when it is revealed she is pregnant by someone—or in this case, something—else. An angel intervenes on her behalf to inform Joseph that the conception was no ordinary event:

> But just when he had resolved to do this, an angel of the Lord appeared to him in a dream and said, "Joseph, son of David, do not be afraid to take Mary as your wife, for the child conceived in her is from the Holy Spirit. She will bear a son, and you are to name him Jesus, for he will save his people from their sins." All this took place to fulfil what had been spoken by the Lord through the prophet: "Look, the virgin shall conceive and bear a son, and they shall name him 'Emmanuel,' which means, 'God is with us.'"[116]

The use of angels by God to provide information on the birth of Jesus is not restricted to this occasion. An angel announces his birth to shepherds, who go to the stable to see what has been proclaimed. In addition, God sends a star to wise men—magi—to inform them of the divine event. They travel from the east and bring portentous gifts of gold, frankincense, and myrrh. With such a divine birth, you might expect that the child will have an exceptional upbringing and show exceptional

---

[116] Matthew 1:20–23.

ability and promise. He might be held in awe by his parents, and he therefore might in effect be spoiled and, if he has godlike ability, misuse it, not yet having the discipline to use his abilities as his Heavenly Father intends. On the other hand, if he is fully divine, he may, from the very beginning, be immune to the foibles of human weaknesses, and be fully able to use his divine attributes without the danger of Ego inflation, which many children raised as semidivine beings by their parents are heir to.

Figure 16 Adoration of the Magi

The birth of Jesus—in lowly estate, in a stable, among animals—does not happen by chance; nothing in the birth narrative does. Jesus, as the archetype of the divine child, is the incarnation of the Self—the God archetype. Edward Edinger explores the significance of this happening among animals in their abode:

> Birth among animals signifies that the coming of the Self is an instinctual process, a part of living nature rooted in the biology of our being. As Jung told a patient, an experience of the transpersonal Self, if it is not to cause inflation, "needs a great humility to counterbalance it. You need to go down to a level of the mice."[117]

As Edinger proposes, Jesus's birth is a balance between the humble and the grand. The stable has two sets of visitors who come to worship the new king of the Jews at the call of the divine. There are the humble shepherds—who were the lowliest of the low in those times—and the wise men, or magi, from the east, who are also transformed into kings by the later mythologizing. This portentous beginning reveals the challenge Jesus will face throughout his life—to maintain that balance and resist the danger of Ego inflation. Unfortunately, the Bible contains only one account of Jesus's exploits when he was a child. This is the account of the events when he visits the temple in Jerusalem at twelve years old:

> Now every year his parents went to Jerusalem for the festival of the Passover. And when he was twelve years old, they went up as usual for the festival. When the festival was ended and they started to return, the boy

---

117 Edinger, *The Christian Archetype*, 14.

> Jesus stayed behind in Jerusalem, but his parents did not know it. Assuming that he was in the group of travellers, they went a day's journey. Then they started to look for him among their relatives and friends. When they did not find him, they returned to Jerusalem to search for him. After three days they found him in the temple, sitting among the teachers, listening to them and asking them questions. And all who heard him were amazed at his understanding and his answers. When his parents saw him they were astonished; and his mother said to him, "Child, why have you treated us like this? Look, your father and I have been searching for you in great anxiety." He said to them, "Why were you searching for me? Did you not know that I must be in my Father's house?' But they did not understand what he said to them. Then he went down with them and came to Nazareth, and was obedient to them. His mother treasured all these things in her heart.[118]

In some ways, this is the account of a typical teenager. He is unmindful of how his actions will affect others—particularly his parents. He is somewhat disdainful of their natural concern for his well-being and dismissive of their authority. On the other hand, the account points to the greatness ahead. At this precocious age he shows great wisdom to the elders at the temple. Finally, we are told that this outburst—if it may be called that—is the exception to his behaviour. From this point on in his childhood, he is obedient to his parents. He shows no sign of the Ego

---

118 Luke 2:41–51.

inflation he could well have been subject to, if he had been a normal child raised in such abnormal circumstances.

As we might expect, of course, there would have been apocryphal stories of the life of a divine child with the potential for divine abilities. One example has him creating living birds out of clay:

> This little child Jesus when he was five years old was playing at the ford of a brook: and he gathered together the waters that flowed there into pools, and made them straightway clean, and commanded them by his word alone. And having made soft clay, he fashioned thereof twelve sparrows. And it was the Sabbath when he did these things (or made them). And there were also many other little children playing with him.[119]

This is a rather harmless, if miraculous, thing that the child Jesus does. He does not, however, obey the commandment to remember the Sabbath and keep it holy. This is an area in which he will run into problems when he reaches his full maturity. However, another example shows him using his divine abilities to less than harmless results:

> After that again he went through the village and a child ran and dashed against his shoulder. And Jesus was provoked and said unto him: Thou shalt not finish thy course (lit. go all thy way). And immediately he fell down and died. But certain when they saw what was done

---

[119] "The Apocryphal New Testament," trans. and notes by M.R. James. Oxford: Clarendon Press, 1924. http://gnosis.org/library/inftoma.htm

said: Whence was this young child born, for that every word of his is an accomplished work? And the parents of him that was dead came unto Joseph, and blamed him, saying: Thou that hast such a child canst not dwell with us in the village: or do thou teach him to bless and not to curse: for he slayeth our children.

And Joseph called the young child apart and admonished him, saying: Wherefore doest thou such things, that these suffer and hate us and persecute us? But Jesus said: I know that these thy words are not thine: nevertheless for thy sake I will hold my peace: but they shall bear their punishment. And straightway they that accused him were smitten with blindness. And they that saw it were sore afraid and perplexed, and said concerning him that every word which he spake whether it were good or bad, was a deed, and became a marvel. And when they [he ?] saw that Jesus had so done, Joseph arose and took hold upon his ear and wrung it sore. And the young child was wroth and said unto him: It sufficeth thee [or them] to seek and not to find, and verily thou hast done unwisely: knowest thou not that I am thine? vex me not.[120]

This shows the havoc that an immature child with an inflated Ego can wreak—particularly if he or she has superhuman abilities. It also indicates the challenges and potential dangers to parents of such a child.

---

120 Ibid.

One might consider that Joseph is walking in a potential minefield by disciplining Jesus. It is commendable that Jesus restrains himself and accepts the punishment—albeit with less than good grace. Jung addresses the embryotic stage of development of the individuation journey that Jesus is apparently experiencing here. I quote at length due to its description of the critical juncture Jesus faces at this point in his journey:

> The initial state of personal infantilism presents the picture of an "abandoned" or "misunderstood" and unjustly treated child with overweening pretensions. The epiphany of the hero (the second identification) shows itself in a corresponding inflation: the colossal pretension grows into a conviction that one is something extraordinary, or else the impossibility of the pretension ever being fulfilled only proves one's own inferiority, which is favourable to the role of the heroic sufferer (a negative inflation). In spite of their contradictoriness, both forms are identical, because conscious megalomania is balanced by unconscious compensatory interiority and conscious inferiority by unconscious megalomania (you never get one without the other). Once the reef of the second identification has been successfully circumnavigated, conscious processes can be cleanly separated for the unconscious and the latter observed objectively. This leads to the possibility of an accommodation with the unconscious, and thus to a possible synthesis of the conscious and unconscious elements of knowledge and

action. This in turn leads to a shifting of the centre of personality from ego to the self.[121]

From this dissertation, we see the incredibly complex and complicated journey that Jesus embarks on. A lesser mortal, one without the advantage of also being fully divine, could easily fall into the traps that are laid by the Ego. However, Jesus has the advantage of that divinity to aid and guide him on his journey to integration with the Self.

We next meet the Jesus of Scripture when he is about to begin his public ministry. It's traditionally thought that he is thirty years old at this point. We do not know what he has been doing since the age of twelve. However, he is now a fully mature man who would likely have been doing the usual things a Jewish man would. He appears to have burst on the scene without previous notoriety, as his ministry is a surprise to many who would have known him. One of his first acts after he begins his public ministry, according to the Gospel of Luke, is to preach in the local synagogue:

> "The Spirit of the Lord is upon me,
>   because he has anointed me
>   to bring good news to the poor.
> He has sent me to proclaim release to the captives
>   and recovery of sight to the blind,
>   to let the oppressed go free,
>   to proclaim the year of the Lord's favour."
> And he rolled up the scroll, gave it back to the attendant, and sat down. The eyes of all in the synagogue

---

121 *The Archetypes and the Collective Unconscious*, 180.

were fixed on him. Then he began to say to them, "Today this scripture has been fulfilled in your hearing."[122]

The reaction of the congregation is telling. "All spoke well of him and were amazed at the gracious words that came from his mouth. They said, 'Is not this Joseph's son?'"[123] In effect, a local man surprises those who know him as a child and young man. Apparently, they are not aware of his apocryphal exploits. However, he makes a public declaration that he is Christ—the one the prophet had foretold. This could be seen as a case of Ego gone completely out of control—a case of megalomania. Today, this would be diagnosed as a messiah complex, the Ego overwhelmed by an unconscious archetype. However, for Christians, it is seen as the first public declaration of who he is and what he has come to be—the messiah. If one truly is the son the God, then he is not under a delusion.

Returning to the beginning of his ministry—or rather as a prelude to it—Jesus appears before his cousin John the Baptist, who is baptizing people for the repentance of sins in the Jordan River. At Jesus's request that John baptize him, John reacts against the idea. "John would have prevented him, saying, 'I need to be baptized by you, and do you come to me?' But Jesus answered him, 'Let it be so now; for it is proper for us in this way to fulfil all righteousness.' Then he consented."[124]

Jesus places himself in a subservient position to John. It would be very easy for him to have consented to John's request to be baptized by

---

122 Luke 4:18–21.
123 Luke 4:22.
124 Matthew 3:14–15.

THE EGO AND THE BIBLE

Jesus, instead of baptizing him. He is aware—or at least has the beginning of awareness—of who he is and what he is on earth to do. However, his Ego is not in control at this time. He has a relationship to God the Father that places the Ego in its proper place—in service to the Self. When Jesus comes up out of the water (John uses full-immersion baptism), he is visited by the third person of the Trinity in the form of a dove consecrating his baptism and his intention to begin his ministry. The voice of the first person of the Trinity confirms this. "The Holy Spirit descended upon him in bodily form like a dove. And a voice came from heaven, 'You are my Son, the Beloved; with you I am well pleased.'"[125]

Figure 17 The Temptation of Christ

---

125   Luke 3:22.

Jesus then needs to sojourn in the wilderness before he begins his ministry. He is sent on this journey by the same Holy Spirit; accounts of this differ. Two Gospel accounts—those of Matthew and Luke—state he is "led" into the wilderness. However, Mark, generally considered the earliest recorder of the Gospel, gives a different perspective. "And the Spirit immediately drove him out into the wilderness."[126] This is an important distinction for our purposes; to be led implies that there is no resistance on Jesus's part. However, to be driven to this trial indicates that the Holy Spirit, whom we must assume knows well its fellow member of the Godhead, is aware that there may well be resistance from Jesus to undertaking this act. Jesus is in danger of Ego inflation as a result of the divine declaration that he is God's son. The temptations that he could experience in his ministry from the adulation that will come to him at times would be hard for his Ego to resist. Therefore, this time in the wilderness is a necessary prelude to this calling. Edward Edinger speaks to this:

> Immediately following the Baptism we read, "Then was Jesus led up of the Spirit into the wilderness to be tempted of the devil." (Matt 4:1) This sequence refers to the danger of inflation that accompanies an encounter with the Self.[127]

The Ego may indeed not want to undertake something it knows is necessary. This is a common occurrence, as people will do things they know are not in their best interest. Even St. Paul, the great evangelist, was

---
126 Mark 1:12.
127 Edinger, *The Christian Archetype*, 53.

THE EGO AND THE BIBLE

well aware of this. "I do not understand my own actions. For I do not do what I want, but I do the very thing I hate."[128] This is an indication that Jesus's Ego is not entirely in service to the Self. It may want to assert itself on this journey that will eventually lead Jesus to Jerusalem and the cross.

Jesus spends the forty-day period in the wilderness. While there, he has what has been described as a spirit walk by North American natives or a walkabout in the Australian Aboriginal tradition. Jesus encounters his erstwhile brother Satan the tempter. Satan offers him three great temptations. First, he suggests that Jesus, who has been without food for the forty days, turn the stones in bread. Jesus famously responds, "It is written, 'One does not live by bread alone, but by every word that comes from the mouth of God.'"[129] Next, the great tempter tempts him to demonstrate God the Father's care for him—he tells Jesus to throw himself off the pinnacle of the temple, for it is written that angels will bear him up. Jesus responds, "Again it is written, 'Do not put the Lord your God to the test.'"[130] Finally, he offers Jesus the greatest temptation, showing Jesus all the kingdoms of the world and offering them to him if he will bow down and worship Satan. Jesus gives his final and absolute response: "Away with you, Satan! for it is written, 'Worship the Lord your God and serve only him.'"[131]

This is the great test of Jesus's Ego-centeredness. Jesus could have succumbed to the temptation that every human is heir to—the desire for

---

128 Romans 7:15.
129 Matthew 4:4.
130 Matthew 4:7.
131 Matthew 4:10.

things that the Ego wants: to meet physical demands and desires, proof that one is the most important thing in his or her parents' lives, and absolute power over our world. This is the critical test—whether Jesus will allow his Ego to rule or, making his Ego serve the Self, follow the path that he has come to earth to follow and fulfil. Jesus makes the critical choice for his Ego to be the servant of the Self. With this decision, Jesus's path is set—one that will inevitably lead him to his cross.

Chapter 18

Mary: The God Bearer

In the sixth month the angel Gabriel was sent by God to a town in Galilee called Nazareth, to a virgin engaged to a man whose name was Joseph, of the house of David. The virgin's name was Mary. And he came to her and said, "Greetings, favoured one! The Lord is with you." But she was much perplexed by his words and pondered what sort of greeting this might be. The angel said to her, "Do not be afraid, Mary, for you have found favour with God. And now, you will conceive in your womb and bear a son, and you will name him Jesus. He will be great, and will be called the Son of the Most High, and the Lord God will give to him the throne of his ancestor David. He will reign over the house of Jacob for ever, and of his kingdom there will be no end." Mary said to the angel, "How can this be, since I am a virgin?" The angel said to her, "The Holy Spirit will come upon you, and the power of the Most High will overshadow you; therefore the child to be born will be holy; he will be called Son of God. And now, your relative Elizabeth in her old age has also conceived a son; and this is the sixth month for her who was said to be barren. For nothing will be impossible with God." Then Mary said, "Here am I, the servant

of the Lord; let it be with me according to your word."
Then the angel departed from her.[132]

With this beginning to the nativity story—the story of the birth of Jesus Christ—Luke's Gospel introduces his readers to the young woman named Mary, who will become a pivotal part of Christian belief. We know little about her, only that she is a young (possibly very young) woman who is betrothed to a man named Joseph.

There is not much in this that gives the reader any indication of what will happen. This lowly young woman receives a revelation from a divine source—the heavenly messenger Gabriel—who has wondrous news for Mary. However, as we have discovered, divine messages are often mixed ones, portents of difficult times ahead for the people receiving them. It is Mary's response that gives us the first indication of why this young woman is chosen by God—chosen to be the one who will carry the incarnate son of God the Father. "Then Mary said, 'Here am I, the servant of the Lord; let it be with me according to your word.'"[133]

---

[132] Luke 1:26–37.
[133] Luke 1:38.

THE EGO AND THE BIBLE

Figure 18 The Annunciation

Despite her caution, as indicated by her reaction to Gabriel's greeting—being much perplexed by his words—she does not hesitate to accept God's intention for her. This action of Mary to accept God's will is quite surprising. Many who have received God's call, before and after Mary, to perform a difficult task have been reluctant undertake it without resistance, at least initially. This is exceptional; the Ego of one so young would not normally be developed to the point where the will of God would be accepted with such seeming ease. As Mary is "much perplexed," this is a strong indication that she would have known what the future was for a woman who became pregnant by someone outside of marriage—or even betrothal—if the father of the child was not the betrothed. She would likely be put to death by stoning, as was required by the law. In an act of deus ex machina, divine intervention saves Mary

MARY: THE GOD BEARER

from the seemingly inevitable fate ordained for an unmarried pregnant woman.

It is interesting that Luke does not deal with the predicament that Mary finds herself in. We must turn to the Gospel of Matthew to get this critical part of the story. If Mary had been left to her apparent fate, the Christ Child would never have survived the pregnancy. Matthew reveals that Mary would not have suffered the usual fate, regardless of divine intervention. Joseph, "being a righteous man and unwilling to expose her to public disgrace, planned to dismiss her quietly."[134] However, Mary is doubly saved by the divine will, as Joseph is also visited by a—this time unnamed—holy messenger, who reveals the divine nature of Mary's predicament. "Joseph, son of David, do not be afraid to take Mary as your wife, for the child conceived in her is from the Holy Spirit."[135]

From these events, we see that the Holy Family will have good start to a challenging adventure. Joseph, exceptional in his kindly attitude toward his betrothed, does not question his unique state—being cuckolded by God. Mary is an exceptional young woman, who has no hesitation in following the divine fate ordained for her; she is truly blessed with a psyche that is not Ego controlled, despite her youth.

Mary continues to show that she is mature, someone whose Ego is basically in service of the Self throughout the trials of her giving birth in trying circumstances and her lowly estate. The birth is appropriately marked with heavenly signs and messengers with wonderful

---
134 Matthew 1:19.
135 Matthew 1:20.

messages—from visits by the lowly shepherds (as reported by Luke) with accounts of heavenly messages, to noble Magi (as reported by Matthew) following stars and bearing portentous gifts. Luke tells us that "Mary treasured all these words and pondered them in her heart."[136] These events are followed by the flight to Egypt to escape the Ego-charged threat from King Herod, who feared the threat of a potential usurper of his throne.

We hear little regarding the life of Mary until Jesus is grown and his public ministry is well launched. There is the account of Jesus's visit to the temple, discussed above. Other than that, we discover Mary through the biblical stories, later assuming the archetypal role of Jewish mother. We see her as someone who is less sure of her role as the mother of God than when she first assumed that divinely ordained role. The Gospel of John records the events at the marriage at Cana, discussed below, when Jesus is put out by Mary's request that he do something about the lack of wine. She is concerned that Jesus, her divinely ordained son, should do something to save the marrying couple from a socially embarrassing situation. We also have the more revealing incident when Jesus's family hear reports that he is out of his mind. "Then he went home; and the crowd came together again, so that they could not even eat. When his family heard it, they went out to restrain him, for people were saying, 'He has gone out of his mind.'"[137] Although this passage does not specify that Mary is on the scene, other sources refer to his mother and brothers. One commentary notes that this is a case

---

136 Luke 2:19.
137 Mark 3:20–21.

where the family seeks to protect Jesus from the rising storm of criticism—in particular, "it is evident that Mary also was drawn into this error of worldly policy."[138]

We can see that Mary did have Ego-based concerns with the actions of her divine son. She cannot completely put her Ego in the service of the Self, even when that image of God is her own son.

In the final events of the story of Mary, we have the heart-rending events at the cross, where Mary witnesses the cruel execution of her son:

> Meanwhile, standing near the cross of Jesus were his mother, and his mother's sister, Mary the wife of Clopas, and Mary Magdalene. When Jesus saw his mother and the disciple whom he loved standing beside her, he said to his mother, "Woman, here is your son." Then he said to the disciple, "Here is your mother." And from that hour the disciple took her into his own home.[139]

Even near death, Jesus shows his love and concern for his mother. He fulfills the role of the responsible male member of the family (we must presume that Joseph has departed the earth for his heavenly reward) and ensured that his mother will be cared for after his death. Here we have an earthly, Ego-based bond that takes precedence over the moment when the Ego of both will be subsumed into the Self.

---

138 http://biblehub.com/commentaries/lange/mark/3.htm
139 John 19:25–27.

THE EGO AND THE BIBLE

The final account of Mary in the Gospels has her at the empty tomb, coming with other women to anoint the body of her son. Here is the final act of devotion of a loving mother for her son. We can only imagine the pain that Mary must have felt, experiencing what appeared to be the final episode in her son's life—one that began so dramatically and must have given her much grief and much joy.

It is interesting that the Gospels do not record that the resurrected Jesus appeared to his mother. This has been the subject of much speculation—particularly on the part of Roman Catholic theologians, given the veneration of Mary by that faith. Going on the basis of Scripture, we can only wonder why this did not occur. Did the Jesus that was now united fully with the Godhead know that this was not necessary for Mary in her postcrucifixion Ego state? We will have to leave Mary with our question unanswered, much to the dissatisfaction of our Ego desires.

Chapter 19

Satan: The Tempter

> How you are fallen from heaven,
>
> O Day Star, son of Dawn!
>
> How you are cut down to the ground,
>
> you who laid the nations low! You said in your heart,
>
> "I will ascend to heaven;
>
> I will raise my throne
>
> above the stars of God;
>
> I will sit on the mount of assembly
>
> on the heights of Zaphon; I will ascend to the tops of the clouds,
>
> I will make myself like the Most High."[140]

Jesus's temptation in the wilderness raises the question of whether Satan indeed possesses an Ego state. Let us leave Jesus for the moment and explore further the character of Satan/the devil. The tempter of Jesus is either Satan (in Mark) or the devil (in Matthew and Luke).

---

140 Isaiah 14:12–14.

Interestingly, there is no account of the temptation in the wilderness in John's Gospel. In the book of Job, it is Satan—the accuser—who is the troublemaker who convinces Yahweh to allow him to test Job's faithfulness. Jesus's adversary is also presented as Lucifer, which means "light bringer" in Latin. There is not a great deal of biblical information about Satan/the devil and how he became Jesus's adversary in the wilderness. In the book of Job, as noted, he is one of the "heavenly beings" in God's heavenly court. However, there are a few clues about how he went from being a royal courtier to being the tempter of Jesus in the wilderness. Jung addresses the concept of Satan/devil as tempter while still being a spirit, i.e., heavenly member of God's court:

> When the Bible says "God is spirit," it sounds like a definition of a substance, or like a qualification. But the devil too, it seems, is endowed with the same particular substance, albeit an evil and corrupt one. The original identity of substance is still expressed in the idea of the fallen angel, as well as in the close connection between Jehovah and Satan in the Old Testament. There may be an echo of this primitive connection in the Lord's Prayer; where we say "Lead us not into temptation"—for is not this really the business of the tempter, the devil himself?[141]

The passage from Isaiah above refers to the star of heaven that has fallen to the ground because of pride and ambition. In addition there is a passage in Ezekiel:

---

141 *The Archetypes and the Collective Unconscious*, 214.

> With an anointed cherub as guardian I placed you;
>
> you were on the holy mountain of God;
>
> you walked among the stones of fire. You were blameless in your ways
>
> from the day that you were created,
>
> until iniquity was found in you. In the abundance of your trade
>
> you were filled with violence, and you sinned;
>
> so I cast you as a profane thing from the mountain of God,
>
> and the guardian cherub drove you out
>
> from among the stones of fire. Your heart was proud because of your beauty;
>
> you corrupted your wisdom for the sake of your splendour.
>
> I cast you to the ground.[142]

Here we have the additional confirmation that Lucifer's wisdom has been corrupted for sake of his splendour. We have the picture of what could be considered the greatest of the heavenly creatures—the most beautiful and luminous; God's golden offspring—at least until the incarnation of the son. There is a rather enigmatic passage in which Jesus refers to Satan's fall. "He said to them, 'I watched Satan fall from heaven like a flash of lightning.'"[143] However, this almost seems out of

---
142 Ezekiel 28:14–17.
143 Luke 10:18.

context. His destiny is addressed in the book of Revelation—he will first be bound for one thousand years by an angel of God:

> Then I saw an angel coming down from heaven, having the key to the bottomless pit and a great chain in his hand. He laid hold of the dragon, that serpent of old, who is the Devil and Satan, and bound him for a thousand years; and he cast him into the bottomless pit, and shut him up, and set a seal on him, so that he should deceive the nations no more till the thousand years were finished. But after these things he must be released for a little while.[144]

Here we have the additional reference to Satan as the serpent of old, which would place him as the serpent in the Garden of Eden, who tempted Eve and, we can infer, Adam. Finally, after the thousand years, he will be released for a short time, only to be ultimately defeated:

> And the devil who had deceived them was thrown into the lake of fire and sulphur, where the beast and the false prophet were, and they will be tormented day and night for ever and ever.[145]

---

[144] Revelation 20:1–3.
[145] Revelation 20:10.

Figure 19 Statue of the Fallen Angel

This is perhaps a fitting end for a being who had caused so much torment to so many and has been a general troublemaker. However, as noted at the beginning of this document, he was a necessity for our first parents if they were going to achieve the God-given gift of consciousness.

The overriding sin of Satan/the Devil/the Great Serpent/ Lucifer was pride. This overarching pride led to his challenge of God, as noted in the Isaiah passage: "I will ascend to the tops of the clouds; I will make myself like the Most High." Similarly, in Ezekiel we are told, "Your heart was proud because of your beauty; you corrupted your wisdom for the sake of your splendour." He, like Narcissus, has the fatal flaw of falling in love with his own reflected glory and believing that his glory is above

THE EGO AND THE BIBLE

even God. In this perspective, the name Lucifer best reflects who he is—at least until the fall.

On this basis, we must conclude that Lucifer does indeed have an Ego. It is his Ego consciousness that is inflated by his pride in his own glory. As Jung noted, "Spirit threatens the naïve-minded man with inflation."[146] Now Lucifer/Satan is certainly not a naïve man, but if the favoured heavenly spirit can suffer from this sin, then humans are certainly subject to it, as Jung notes. The classic saying "pride goeth before a fall" is particularly apt here and is possibly based on the myth of Lucifer's fall from heaven. It is certainly part of wisdom literature as found in Proverbs 16:18: "Pride goes before destruction and a haughty spirit before a fall."

Pride is one of the classic seven deadly sins, or mortal sins, as they are termed today by the Roman Catholic Church. It can and does lead to Ego inflation, as we can see in Lucifer and as is well stated recently in a sermon—"Pride builds walls around our hearts."[147] It is the opposite of compassion, which opens the heart to God's creation. Lucifer can never be accused of having compassion.

---

146 *The Phenomenon of the Spirit, Fairytales* in *The Archetypes of the Collective Unconscious*, 213.
147 From an unpublished sermon by Dr. Joe Corcoran delivered in the chapel of Huron University College, London, Ontario, Jan. 22, 2014.

Chapter 20

Jesus: From Wilderness to the Cross

Let us turn back to Jesus now that we have considered both his dark and bright shadow in the person of Satan/Lucifer. When we left Jesus, he was in the wilderness encountering the temptations of the Ego presented by Satan/Lucifer. Jesus returns from the trial and purification experience of the wilderness prepared to begin his public ministry.

The Gospel accounts differ in how this ministry begins. In Matthew, Mark, and Luke—the synoptic Gospels—he begins by either calling his first disciples or proclaiming, in the synagogue or its vicinity, that the Kingdom of God is at hand. In these cases, we see that the Ego of Jesus is working in the service of the Self—the God within. His face is set on what he understands to be his mission and purpose—why God the Father has incarnated him. There is no evidence that the motivation for this is Ego based—he has received the anointing by the Holy Spirit at his baptism and been purified in the wilderness. He is on the path that the divinity has set for him.

The account in the Gospel of John differs in many ways from the synoptic Gospels. The account of Jesus's embarkation into ministry is no different. He initially calls two disciples, albeit not fishermen. However, the next events set the account on a much different course. In John,

THE EGO AND THE BIBLE

immediately after calling the disciples, Jesus attends a wedding at Cana, where he performs his first miracle—not counting the noncanonical, brash ones of his childhood. This is where Jesus steps in to save the marriage couple from the extreme embarrassment of running out of wine during the wedding banquet. He changes the water used for purification rites into wine. In this act, he responds to his mother's implied request that he should fix the problem:

> When the wine gave out, the mother of Jesus said to him, "They have no wine." And Jesus said to her, "Woman, what concern is that to you and to me? My hour has not yet come." His mother said to the servants, "Do whatever he tells you."[148]

In his response to his mother, there seems to be a lack of compassion for the people involved in the wedding. There is also perhaps a hint of annoyance, which one can imagine in his voice; i.e., "Mother, don't bother me with such trivial matters when I have more important things to consider." This perhaps shows a lack of compassion toward his host. Possibly Jesus's Ego is not entirely in the service of the Self. He has some Ego involvement with his mission. The next event in John's Gospel is Jesus cleansing the temple of the money changers. This event occurs out of sync with the synoptic Gospels, where it occurs after the triumphal entry into Jerusalem. For John, this event is connected to the miracle of the wine, and there does seem to be a connection in terms of Jesus acting out of what we generally think of as his character of compassion and love. I will delve into this at length later.

---

148 John 2:3–5.

Let us look at other times when Jesus seems to act out of his general character of compassion. Jesus does have a general attitude of condemnation for the Pharisees and other religious leaders. An example of this is in Matthew:

> Then Jesus spoke to the multitudes and to His disciples, saying: "The scribes and the Pharisees sit in Moses' seat. Therefore whatever they tell you to observe, that observe and do, but do not do according to their works; for they say, and do not do. For they bind heavy burdens, hard to bear, and lay them on men's shoulders; but they themselves will not move them with one of their fingers. But all their works they do to be seen by men.[149]

This attitude of Jesus's—though rather severe—is not out of proportion to what the Pharisees deserved, and it can be seen as justified. Reactions that are out of proportion are evidence that a complex or projection is involved. So, let's set this aside and look for other situations. Matthew and Mark tell of Jesus's encounter with the Canaanite woman who approaches Jesus to perform an exorcism on her daughter, who is tormented by a demon. The woman approaches Jesus in what can be considered reverence, but also desperation. "Just then a Canaanite woman from that region came out and started shouting, 'Have mercy on me, Lord, Son of David; my daughter is tormented by a demon.'"[150] However, Jesus's response is to ignore her. In her desperation she persists and Jesus gives this response:

---

149 Matthew 23:1–5.
150 Matthew 15:22.

> He answered, "I was sent only to the lost sheep of the house of Israel." But she came and knelt before him, saying, "Lord, help me.'" He answered, "It is not fair to take the children's food and throw it to the dogs."[151]

This is similar to, but more extreme than, his response to his mother at Cana. He has no time for these distractions from his mission. There is no compassion in his response to this woman who throws herself at his feet. Rather, there is no compassion until she continues to persist: "She said, 'Yes, Lord, yet even the dogs eat the crumbs that fall from their masters' table.'"[152] At this, he responds in a way similar to how he responds to the request by his mother; he shows compassion for the other. It is as if he is awakened from a complex that has possession of his consciousness.

Another example that is closer to home for Jesus, in his attitude toward his family, involves his mother and brothers coming to see him:

> Then his mother and his brothers came to him, but they could not reach him because of the crowd. And he was told, "Your mother and your brothers are standing outside, wanting to see you." But he said to them, "My mother and my brothers are those who hear the word of God and do it."[153]

This event is also recorded in Matthew and Mark. There is a legitimate theological perspective on this—Jesus wants to make the point

---

151 Matthew 25:24–26.
152 Matthew 15:27.
153 Luke 8:19–22.

that family will sometimes or even often stand in the way of a person's true calling. However, you must wonder at the apparent disregard for those closest to him—especially his mother Mary, who risked so much to bear him. Could he not have made his point without it being at the expense of his family? Again, we have to suspect that his Ego is, at least in part, tied up with his mission in a less than positive way.

Now let us return to the events surrounding the cleansing of the temple. As noted above in all the Gospels except John, this event closely follows Jesus's triumphal entry into Jerusalem. Matthew records the event thus:

> When they came near Jerusalem and had reached Bethphage, at the Mount of Olives, Jesus sent two disciples, saying to them, "Go into the village ahead of you, and immediately you will find a donkey tied, and a colt with her; untie them and bring them to me. If anyone says anything to you, just say this, 'The Lord needs them.' And he will send them immediately." This took place to fulfil what had been spoken through the prophet, saying, "Tell the daughter of Zion, Look, your king is coming to you, humble, and mounted on a donkey, and on a colt, the foal of a donkey."
>
> The disciples went and did as Jesus had directed them; they brought the donkey and the colt, and put their cloaks on them, and he sat on them. A very large crowd

spread their cloaks on the road, and others cut branches from the trees and spread them on the road. The crowds that went ahead of him and that followed were shouting,

"Hosanna to the Son of David!

Blessed is the one who comes in the name of the Lord!

Hosanna in the highest heaven!"[154]

There can be no mistake that in this act Jesus is declaring himself to be the messiah. This is a direct fulfilment of the prophecy in Zechariah 9:9:

Rejoice greatly, O daughter Zion!
    Shout aloud, O daughter Jerusalem!
Lo, your king comes to you;
    triumphant and victorious is he,
humble and riding on a donkey,
    on a colt, the foal of a donkey.

---

[154] Matthew 21:1–9.

Figure 20 Jesus enters Jerusalem and the crowds welcome him

Certainly this would be evident to the religious leaders and many people in the crowd who were shouting Hosanna. There is no doubt in the Gospel writer's account that this is a fulfilment of the prophecy—this undoubtedly was Jesus's destiny. However, he made a conscious choice to fulfil that prophecy in a way that cannot be denied. In effect, the temptation to take earthly power has overcome his Ego. Edinger address this: "At this moment he succumbs to the power temptation and allows himself to be hailed as a king."[155] This seems counter to his intended purpose. He has declared to his disciples that he is going to Jerusalem to die, as recorded in the three synoptic Gospels. Matthew's version states:

---

155 *The Christian Archetype,* 57.

THE EGO AND THE BIBLE

> From that time on, Jesus began to show his disciples that he must go to Jerusalem and undergo great suffering at the hands of the elders and chief priests and scribes, and be killed, and on the third day be raised.[156]

Indeed when his closest disciple, Peter, asserts that he must not let this happen, Jesus declares in an unusual outburst, "Get behind me, Satan! You are a stumbling-block to me; for you are setting your mind not on divine things but on human things."[157] The strength of this outburst indicates that Peter has hit a hot-button issue for Jesus. This is surprising particularly because it directly follows Jesus's praise of Peter for declaring him the messiah: "And Jesus answered him, 'Blessed are you, Simon son of Jonah! For flesh and blood has not revealed this to you, but my Father in heaven.'"[158] He is not secure in his decision to meet the destiny of the cross—his Ego is struggling against this decision.

Following the triumphal entry in Jerusalem and the declaration by the crowd of Jesus's kingship, Jesus is completely consumed by the power complex and acts out this state by his cleansing of the temple, as noted by Edinger: "And no sooner does he enter Jerusalem than he falls into a rage."[159] This act of violence runs completely against his abhorrence of violence, his prohibition against anger, and his admonition to turn the other cheek, go the second mile, and love not only your neighbour but

---

[156] Matthew 16:21.
[157] Matthew 16:23.
[158] Matthew 17:17.
[159] *The Christian Archetype,* 58.

your enemy. "But I say to you that if you are angry with a brother or sister, you will be liable to judgement."[160]

The mood in which Jesus acts out in his anger continues with his cursing of the fig tree, which has no fruit for him:

> And seeing a fig tree by the side of the road, he went to it and found nothing at all on it but leaves. Then he said to it, "May no fruit ever come from you again!" And the fig tree withered at once.[161]

As Edinger concludes:

> Overt identification with an archetypal image (messianic king) is exceedingly dangerous and yet Christ's identity seems to require it as the dark aspect of the incarnation process. His anger against the money changers violates his own injunction against anger and indicates that "money" was an aspect of his shadow.[162]

Jesus is indeed tempting fate to play into this archetype. However, as we shall see, the Ego's service to the Self does ultimately succeed. The next milestone on Jesus's journey of individuation is the Last Supper. However, prior to this event, which is the foundation of Christian liturgy, we must explore the events surrounding Judas, who is the great betrayer.

---

160 Matthew 5:22.
161 Matthew 21: 19.
162 *The Christian Archetype*, 58.

Chapter 21

Judas: Betrayer or Servant

> Then Satan entered into Judas called Iscariot, who was one of the twelve; he went away and conferred with the chief priests and officers of the temple police about how he might betray him to them.[163]

The betrayal of Judas is recorded in all the Gospels. However, the account in Luke provides a different perspective on the act. Luke provides a reason for this happening—the culprit being the old tempter and deceiver Satan. In the modern take by the comedian Flip Wilson, "The devil made me do it." The Gospels of Matthew and Mark put it down to pure greed—he does it for the thirty pieces of silver offered by the religious authorities, who must have been particularly eager to rid themselves of the potentially dangerous and charismatic messianic figure who had been declared "king of the Jews." The question for us is: What role, if any, does Ego play in this infamous act?

If the motive was purely greed, which in my view is unlikely, it is just a question of the Ego's desire for material goods. Greed is unlikely, because to respond to Jesus's call to follow him was not something that a person concerned with material possessions would have accepted or even considered. Becoming fishers of men does not usually

---

163 Luke 22:3–4.

produce material wealth—or at least doesn't until the era of TV evangelists. However, unlike with some of the other disciples, we know nothing about Judas prior to him becoming a disciple. If he has been possessed by Satan, as specified in the Gospel of Luke, this will be a case of the Ego being subsumed into the power of the spirit of Satan and no longer being in control or having any illusion of being in control.

Figure 21 Kiss of Judas

One theory holds that Judas's action can be called the messianic imperative. Judas could possibly have wanted to force Jesus's hand in bringing about the kingdom of God on earth by leading a revolt against the Roman occupiers. In this scenario, Judas would have been seeking power, albeit on behalf of Jesus. He believed that power should be realized on earth in his time and not in God's time. This scenario has Judas being influenced by desire for power and control, which is a sure sign that the Ego is attempting to rule.

This would fit with the messianic imperative of Judas wanting to force Jesus's hand and believing he could call on his followers to bring about the kingdom. However, as we know from his testimony before Pontius Pilate, he will not follow this path:

> Jesus answered, "My kingdom is not from this world. If my kingdom were from this world, my followers would be fighting to keep me from being handed over to the Jews. But as it is, my kingdom is not from here."[164]

The noncanonical Gospel of Judas, which is dated from possibly the second century C.E., presents Judas as Jesus's truest disciple. The Gospel presents Jesus asking Judas to betray him. As explained by Bart Ehrman:

> For in this Gospel Judas is the only disciple who understands who Jesus really is, and he is the only disciple to whom Jesus delivers his secret revelation that can lead to salvation. The other disciples worship the God of the Old Testament, and so are "ministers of error." Because Judas knows the truth, he performs the greatest service for Jesus: handing him over to be executed so the divine being within Jesus can escape the trappings of his material body. Or as Jesus puts it so cogently in this gospel: "You

---

164 John 18:36.

> (Judas) will exceed all of them [i.e., the other disciples].
> For you will sacrifice the man that clothes me."[165]

This gnostic take on the motivation of Judas would put him in a position of service to the Self—the God Image in Jesus. His Ego would not have been the motivating factor in this action. The canonical Gospel of Matthew gives an account of Judas's death in which he repents when Jesus is condemned, tries to return his blood money, and commits suicide:

> When Judas, his betrayer, saw that Jesus was condemned, he repented and brought back the thirty pieces of silver to the chief priests and the elders. He said, "I have sinned by betraying innocent blood." But they said, "What is that to us? See to it yourself." Throwing down the pieces of silver in the temple, he departed; and he went and hanged himself.[166]

This act of repentance and deep regret would imply that Judas realizes that whatever his motive, be it greed or desire for power or following Jesus's great plan, he can no longer live with the results. His Ego cannot sustain his position in life, and so he gives himself over to fate and judgement, whether it is to occur in hell, as portrayed by Dante, or in heaven.

---

165 *The Gospel of Judas,* 91.
166 Matthew 27:3–5.

Chapter 22

Jesus: From Last Supper to Triumph

> Jesus, knowing that the Father had given all things into his hands, and that he had come from God and was going to God, got up from the table, took off his outer robe, and tied a towel around himself. Then he poured water into a basin and began to wash the disciples' feet and to wipe them with the towel that was tied around him.[167]

Jesus gathers with his disciples for a last meal together in this stage of his journey to union with the Self. His first act, as recorded in the Gospel of John, is to wash the feet of the disciples. This act is not recorded in the synoptic Gospels. However, this act has become very important in the liturgy of the church, being celebrated in the Christian world on Maundy Thursday. This act of humility and service would normally be performed by a servant or slave. It is unheard of that the host would perform such an act. By taking this act upon himself, Jesus moves beyond identification with the archetypal image of the messianic king. His face is turned toward the cross and his Ego is now (almost) completely in the service of the Self. He demonstrates to the

---

167   John 13: 3–5.

disciples that in God's Kingdom, the worldly order will be turned on its head:

> After he had washed their feet, had put on his robe, and had returned to the table, he said to them, "Do you know what I have done to you? You call me Teacher and Lord—and you are right, for that is what I am. So if I, your Lord and Teacher, have washed your feet, you also ought to wash one another's feet. For I have set you an example, that you also should do as I have done to you."[168]

There is no Ego in this act. It is his final attempt to teach his disciples what the Kingdom of God will be, once it is established. It will occur when the Ego is no longer attempting to be in control and be the centre of the individual but rather exists completely in the service of the Self.

The reaction of his most fervent disciple, Peter, whom he calls his rock, is most revealing in terms of Peter's Ego. He cannot bear to see Jesus in the role of the servant, in spite of all Jesus has tried to show and teach him:

> He came to Simon Peter, who said to him, "Lord, are you going to wash my feet?" Jesus answered, "You do not know now what I am doing, but later you will understand." Peter said to him, "You will never wash my feet." [169]

Jesus answers him in a way that finally gets it through to him (I am tempted to say "gets through his thick skull," but that would be unfair

---

168 John 13:12–15.
169 John 13:6.

THE EGO AND THE BIBLE

to one on whom Jesus founded his church). Peter, speaking very much from his emotions and not his head, responds in the all-or-nothing way of one who is in the thrall of his emotions and his unconscious:

> Jesus answered, "Unless I wash you, you have no share with me." Simon Peter said to him, "Lord, not my feet only but also my hands and my head!" Jesus said to him, "One who has bathed does not need to wash, except for the feet, but is entirely clean. And you are clean, though not all of you." For he knew who was to betray him; for this reason he said, "Not all of you are clean."[170]

Peter will soon face his own trial when his own Ego-based fear of annihilation will lead him to deny his master. His Ego is not yet mature enough to travel the path that Jesus travels.

Jesus's next step along the path to union with his Heavenly Father is the crisis in the Garden of Gethsemane. Jesus is faced with the awful truth of what lies ahead of him. He has come to the secluded place with his disciples to pray. He withdraws to even deeper seclusion, taking his inner circle of Peter, James, and John—who have been with him for the most critical times. And yet, they cannot stay awake while he prays, as he requests. Edinger addresses this seeming lack of fortitude on the part of his closest and dearest followers:

> The message seems to be that to survive the conflict between the opposites one must either sleep or pray. As

---

170 John 13:8b–13.

> a psychological procedure prayer corresponds to active imagination, whereby one seeks to bring into visibility the psychic image or fantasy that lies behind the conflict of affects. The emerging image often has a redeeming or transforming effect which reconciles the confliction opposites.[171]

The sleepiness of the three disciples shows that they are not yet conscious enough to encounter the tension of opposites, with which Jesus is now fully engaged. Jesus is therefore alone to face the reality of his terrible fate. Crucifixion was one of the cruelest forms of execution utilized by the Roman Empire; they employed it to ensure that the conquered peoples would not take lightly the consequences of any attempt to overthrow their conquerors. Edinger notes that the horrors of crucifixion are symbolized by the cup that Jesus prays his Heavenly Father will remove from him. "He said, 'Abba, Father, for you all things are possible; remove this cup from me; yet, not what I want, but what you want.'"[172] Edinger notes that to drink the dregs of the cup of Yahweh's wrath means psychologically, "that it is the ego's task in individuation to assimilate the effects of the primordial psyche."[173] Jesus's Ego is torn between wanting the survival of the person, which is its basic primordial imperative, and the goal of the individuation journey, which is to serve the Self.

Jesus is now prepared to face the trial that lies ahead of him—he faces those who will come to arrest him, and he will be betrayed by one of

---

171 *The Christian Archetype*, 73.
172 Mark 14:36.
173 *The Christian Archetype*, 72.

his own, Judas. Jesus faces two "trials," one before the Council of the Sanhedrin—the religious rulers—and the trial before Pontius Pilate, the Roman governor. This amounts to, in effect, a trial by the religious court and a trial before the civil court. Jesus is facing judgement by all the earthly authorities that matter in his world. When he faces the religious court, he, in effect, condemns himself by his own words:

> Then the high priest stood up before them and asked Jesus, "Have you no answer? What is it that they testify against you?" But he was silent and did not answer. Again the high priest asked him, "Are you the Messiah, the Son of the Blessed One?" Jesus said, "I am; and
> 'you will see the Son of Man
> seated at the right hand of the Power,'
> and 'coming with the clouds of heaven.'" [174]

Here we have the statement of a fully individuated person. His identification with the archetypal image of the "Son of Man," the messiah, is not a case of Ego inflation, as it can be with someone who is overwhelmed with a messiah complex. His Ego is in complete service to the Self, and he is living in a state in which his body is of no consequence to him. He realizes that a terrible ordeal faces him, one that will lead to his death by crucifixion. He has passed the crisis he experienced in the Garden and his face is turned toward the final destination of his journey—union with the Godhead.

The result of the civil trial before the Roman governor is predictable. Although Pilate is sympathetic to Jesus and tries to find a way to let

---

[174] Mark 14:60–62.

Jesus avoid his fate, Jesus says nothing in his own defence. The Gospel of John captures the essence of Jesus at this stage:

> Jesus answered, "My kingdom is not from this world. If my kingdom were from this world, my followers would be fighting to keep me from being handed over to the Jews. But as it is, my kingdom is not from here." Pilate asked him, "So you are a king?" Jesus answered, "You say that I am a king. For this I was born, and for this I came into the world, to testify to the truth. Everyone who belongs to the truth listens to my voice." Pilate asked him, "What is truth?"[175]

Pilate's question is left unanswered, likely because Jesus knows that there is no point in responding, as Pilate will not understand. Jesus is now truly "the truth, the light, and the way." He has travelled to the edge of complete union with the Godhead and has given people the model for what it means to follow the path of individuation. This is the truth that Jesus is speaking of.

> Then the soldiers led him into the courtyard of the palace (that is, the governor's headquarters); and they called together the whole cohort. And they clothed him in a purple cloak; and after twisting some thorns into a crown, they put it on him. And they began saluting him, "Hail, King of the Jews!" They struck his head with a reed, spat upon him, and knelt down in homage to him.

---

[175] John 18:36–38.

After mocking him, they stripped him of the purple cloak and put his own clothes on him. Then they led him out to crucify him.[176]

Figure 22 The Mocking of Christ

The torture of Jesus prior to his crucifixion is short and brutal—he is first mocked by soldiers who stage a farcical reenactment of the triumphal entry into Jerusalem. They then turn him into a "clown king," clothing him in the royal purple of a king and crowning him with a crown of thorns. The mocking continues as they strike him with reeds, instead of waving palm branches in his path. It is notable that the Gospel writer does not record any reaction by Jesus. It is as though his Ego-centered

---

176 Mark 15:16–20.

body has become unimportant and of no consequence to either Jesus or the reader.

> When it was noon, darkness came over the whole land until three in the afternoon. At three o'clock Jesus cried out with a loud voice, "Eloi, Eloi, lema sabachthani?" which means, "My God, my God, why have you forsaken me?" When some of the bystanders heard it, they said, "Listen, he is calling for Elijah." And someone ran, filled a sponge with sour wine, put it on a stick, and gave it to him to drink, saying, "Wait, let us see whether Elijah will come to take him down." Then Jesus gave a loud cry and breathed his last. And the curtain of the temple was torn in two, from top to bottom. Now when the centurion, who stood facing him, saw that in this way he breathed his last, he said, "Truly this man was God's Son!"[177]

With the crucifixion, Jesus's connection with his earthly body ends. His Ego-centered consciousness has one last gasp, asserting itself in the agony of abandonment. This is the ultimate defeat of the Ego in the encounter with the Self. The ultimate defeat will lead to the ultimate victory—the resurrection of a spiritual body where the Ego consciousness is truly no longer a factor. The Ego has been completely joined with the Self. It is not a case of being in service to the Self; the journey of individuation has ended with the union with the Self, and the Godhead is now complete and perfect.

---

[177] Mark 15:33–39.

> When the Sabbath was over, Mary Magdalene, and Mary the mother of James, and Salome bought spices, so that they might go and anoint him. And very early on the first day of the week, when the sun had risen, they went to the tomb. They had been saying to one another, "Who will roll away the stone for us from the entrance to the tomb?" When they looked up, they saw that the stone, which was very large, had already been rolled back. As they entered the tomb, they saw a young man, dressed in a white robe, sitting on the right side; and they were alarmed. But he said to them, "Do not be alarmed; you are looking for Jesus of Nazareth, who was crucified. He has been raised; he is not here. Look, there is the place they laid him. But go, tell his disciples and Peter that he is going ahead of you to Galilee; there you will see him, just as he told you." So they went out and fled from the tomb, for terror and amazement had seized them; and they said nothing to anyone, for they were afraid.[178]

As is noted, some ancient authorities end the Gospel of Mark, generally recognized as the earliest Gospel, at this point with the two Marys and Salome fleeing from the empty tomb in terror. The other alternate endings to Mark and the other Gospels fill in the picture for the reader and do not leave us with the terrible state of emptiness in our psyches to match the empty tomb.

---

178 Mark 16:1–8.

However, there is a deep truth in the terror of the empty tomb. We who are still on our journey of individuation must live the tension between our Ego-centered consciousness and the journey in which we have glimpses of the union Jesus models for us. Terror, which the Ego feels when faced with change, and the awe-fullness experienced when we glimpse the Self, is with us. We are called to live in that Divinely Intended Tension of opposites, which, if we persevere, will produce the transcendence that comes from God.

Chapter 23

Paul: Founder of Christianity

Our story of Divine Intention could end here. However, for it to be finished today (it is never complete), let us look at the man who carried the message of Jesus Christ as the divine Son of God to the world.

> That day a severe persecution began against the church in Jerusalem, and all except the apostles were scattered throughout the countryside of Judea and Samaria. Devout men buried Stephen and made loud lamentation over him. But Saul was ravaging the church by entering house after house; dragging off both men and women, he committed them to prison.[179]

We are introduced to Saul, the man who will become Paul, in this short, cryptic passage, which is almost treated as a throwaway comment. Luke, the author of the Acts of the Apostles, could well have said, "Oh, by the way, there is this guy named Saul who is causing us a lot of trouble, throwing the followers of Jesus Christ into prison." We don't hear anything more about this troublesome zealot until, after an interlude, we are told of his trip to Damascus:

---

[179] Acts 8:1–3.

Meanwhile Saul, still breathing threats and murder against the disciples of the Lord, went to the high priest and asked him for letters to the synagogues at Damascus, so that if he found any who belonged to the Way, men or women, he might bring them bound to Jerusalem. Now as he was going along and approaching Damascus, suddenly a light from heaven flashed around him. He fell to the ground and heard a voice saying to him, "Saul, Saul, why do you persecute me?" He asked, "Who are you, Lord?" The reply came, "I am Jesus, whom you are persecuting. But get up and enter the city, and you will be told what you are to do." The men who were travelling with him stood speechless because they heard the voice but saw no one. Saul got up from the ground, and though his eyes were open, he could see nothing; so they led him by the hand and brought him into Damascus. For three days he was without sight, and neither ate nor drank.[180]

---

180 Act 9:1–9.

THE EGO AND THE BIBLE

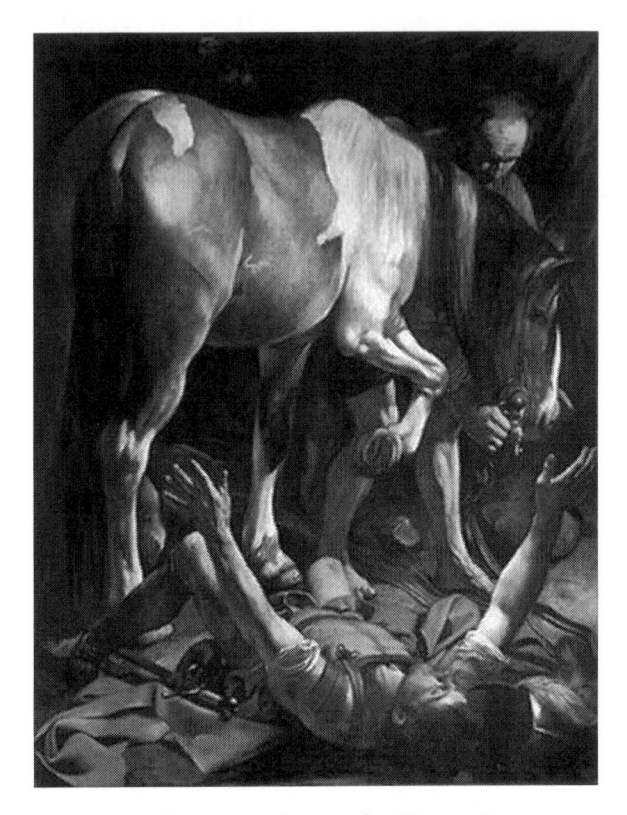

Figure 23 The Conversion on the Way to Damascus

Saul is graphically described by Luke as "breathing threats and murder" against the followers of Jesus Christ. He is on his way to Damascus to continue his "good work" against the apostate Jews, who claim Jesus as the Messiah. However, his journey is rudely interrupted by a light show in the sky and a voice proclaiming, "Saul, Saul, why do you persecute me?"[181] Saul is literally struck blind by the voice, which has self-identified as the same Jesus Christ whose followers he persecuted. After a period of—appropriately—three days, he is able to see the light, literally and

---

181 Acts 9:4.

PAUL: FOUNDER OF CHRISTIANITY

figuratively. He becomes an apostle who outdoes the other apostles—one of the primary evangelizers and main influences in the shape of what will be the early Christian church. Now named Paul, he obtains permission to evangelize Gentiles, founding churches in Asia Minor and, most importantly, to allow them to convert to Christianity without becoming Jews. The will make the new faith much more attractive to non-Jews. The Gentile converts will not be required to be circumcised or follow Jewish dietary practices.

From this, we can see that Paul is someone who identifies strongly with his belief system. He is a Pharisee—part of a Jewish sect that took seriously the call for Jews to fulfil the covenant with Yahweh and follow the commandments. Paul's sense of himself and who he is therefore is joined at the hip to his beliefs. Paul's Ego is completely identified with his persona, and he cannot see himself as anything else. He is fully committed and cannot tolerate a breach of duty by fellow Jews. This upstart group that commits heresy by proclaiming as the Messiah a rabbi who had been ignominiously executed, with common criminals, by the Roman authorities has to be stamped out.

The concept, developed by Jung, of enantiodromia is applicable to Paul's experience. Enantiodromia, in Jung's terms, is the production of an opposite to balance out an extreme position. John P. Dourley, a Jungian analyst and Roman Catholic priest, discusses this in relation to Paul's Damascus road experience: "Revelation would be what occurs when the collective unconscious proffers a new truth to consciousness, in order to compensate an unhealthy one-sidedness."[182]

---

[182] Dourley, *The Illness That We Are*, 28.

THE EGO AND THE BIBLE

Jung comments on the experience of a patient in very different circumstances, which are very applicable here. He notes that "the patient's association to lightning was that it stands for intuition, a conjecture that is not far off the mark, since intuition often comes 'like a flash.'"[183] In Paul's case, the intuition is an overwhelming encounter between the Ego and the Self that literally knocks him to the ground. Jung also notes, in the same source, "The unconscious goes straight for its goal... in allowing an individual to become whole."[184] The divine intercedes in the life of Paul to launch him on his journey of individuation, in which the Ego can ultimately serve the Self rather than itself. It is literally a case of deus ex machina, in which, as Jung notes, the Ego is thrust aside and room is made for the totality of the person. The question before us is as follows: To what extent does Paul travel along the road to individuation?

Paul's life after his encounter with the risen Jesus Christ, albeit in purely spiritual form, reflects his total commitment to evangelizing and spreading the good news of Jesus Christ. He developed a theology that was not based on the life and works of Jesus. This is perhaps not surprising for someone who has not had a face-to-face meeting with either the pre- or postresurrection Jesus. Paul does not speak at any length, in any of his writings, about the person of Jesus who became the Christ. Rather, he develops a theology of Jesus Christ based on faith—the justification by faith in Jesus Christ, in which people can be saved from sin by believing in Jesus Christ. In effect, Paul is creating a church based on

---

183 *Archetypes of the Collective Unconscious*, 303.
184 Ibid.

his mythos of Christ. There is no need for the logos of the facts of Jesus Christ. That would come later with the Gospels, which are set down after Paul writes his letters to the churches he establishes in Corinth and other cities in Asia Minor. It seems that Paul has replaced his original one-sidedness as a committed Pharisee with one-sidedness as the Apostle of Jesus Christ.

In all this, Paul lets it all hang out—his strengths and weaknesses are there for all to read. He notes the struggles he encounters in living by his faith in the statement "I do not understand my own actions. For I do not do what I want, but I do the very thing I hate."[185] From this, we can see that Paul is beset by internal struggles, which may have been the very human conflict between his ideals to live up to his beliefs and the failings of his Ego to follow through with his intentions. Charles Williams has described this as the old self in the new way. Williams explains:

> For the new self does not know itself. It consists of the existence of the self, unselfish perhaps, but not yet denied. This self often applies itself unselfishly. It transfers its activities from itself unselfishly as a centre to its belief as a centre. It uses its angers on behalf of its religion of its morals, and its greed and fear and its pride. It operates on behalf of its notion of God as it originally operated on behalf of itself. It aims honestly at better behaviour, but it does not usually aim at change.[186]

---

185 Romans 7:15.
186 *He Came Down From Heaven*, 85

THE EGO AND THE BIBLE

He has no hesitation to redefine himself as an apostle, who has seen the risen Christ,

> Last of all, as to someone untimely born, he appeared also to me. For I am the least of the apostles, unfit to be called an apostle, because I persecuted the church of God. But by the grace of God I am what I am, and his grace towards me has not been in vain. On the contrary, I worked harder than any of them—though it was not I, but the grace of God that is with me. Whether then it was I or they, so we proclaim and so you have come to believe.[187]

Paul here shows perhaps false modesty and belittles the old self (not in Jung's sense of the Self) but to uphold himself as the one who works "harder than any of them." In this he holds himself to be the greatest of the apostles. He also has no problem telling of his attributes, of course always giving the credit to God:

> Look at what is before your eyes. If you are confident that you belong to Christ, remind yourself of this, that just as you belong to Christ, so also do we. Now, even if I boast a little too much of our authority, which the Lord gave for building you up and not for tearing you down, I will not be ashamed of it. I do not want to seem as though I am trying to frighten you with my letters. For they say, "His letters are weighty and strong, but his

---

[187] I Corinthians 15:8–11.

bodily presence is weak, and his speech contemptible." Let such people understand that what we say by letter when absent, we will also do when present.[188]

In all this we can see that Paul is a very complex and complicated person. There is no doubt he was committed to spreading the Gospel of his personal myth of Jesus Christ; he suffers hardship and is persecuted by the authorities. He is in jail many times and, by his own admission, is severely abused during these times. In all this, he is very successful in evangelizing the Gentile world, and he establishes churches in Asia Minor. However, in all this we see evidence that he was operating from an Ego-centered position. It was his personal vision of Christ that dominated, and he did not suffer any other vision or version to contaminate his Truth. He was, in Charles Williams's words, truly an old self in the new way. Although he committed much to the new way, it was ultimately from the old Ego-based centre.

---

[188] 2 Corinthians 10:7–11.

Conclusion

Christian and Jewish Holy Scripture tells us that humankind is created in God's image—male and female He created us. The essence of that God Image is the gift of consciousness and Ego. As Ego-bearing beings, we have the ultimate gift of knowing that we are separate, unique creations of our creator. We know that we are separate from God but also that we are able to make the journey of individuation throughout our lives. During this journey, we will be drawn closer to that ultimate union with God, which will happen when our time on this earth has run its course.

The God-given gift of Ego had a great impact on the people of Holy Scripture and played a great role in the journeys of those individuals in their relationship to the divine. Our lives can be and are similarly influenced by our Egos, for good and for ill. The impact of our Ego on our journey is entirely dependent on our relation to the psychic energy God gives to us. It is my hope that the accounts that have been explored here will help you on your journey.

It is through our journey of individuation that we will find the laughter at the heart of things, as has been proclaimed by Helen Luke and others. We will learn that all the efforts of our Egos were but a preliminary to the great joy that we will experience in even a small glimpse of that great union with God.

About the Author

Before becoming a priest in the Anglican Church of Canada, the Reverend Greg Little was a career civil servant in the Ontario government for thirty years. During that time, he earned a BA from the University of Toronto. Much later, he pursued his MDiv at Huron University College in London, Ontario, which then launched him into ordained ministry.

Having long had an interest in Jungian dream work, Little studied at the Haden Institute, and as a graduate of their Dream Leader program, has conducted workshops exploring dreams in a group process and led ongoing dream groups.

Now retired from parish work, he recently completed the Haden Institute's joint Spiritual Direction program at Mt. Carmel Spiritual Centre and serves as a spiritual director who incorporates dreams into different aspects of his practice.

In his debut book, *The Ego and the Bible*, Little examines the stories of major biblical characters from a Jungian perspective.

Bibliography

Clasper, Paul, *Eastern Paths and the Christian Way*, Orbis Books Maryknoll NY 1980

Dourley, John. *The Illness That We Are* Inner City Books, Toronto 1984

Edinger, Edward. *The Christian Archetype, Inner* City Books Toronto 1987

Edinger, Edward. *The Bible and The Psyche, Inner* City Books Toronto 1986

Edinger, Edward. *The Encounter with the Self, Inner* City Books Toronto 1986

Holy Bible, New Revised Standard Version

Jung, C. G. Mysterium Coniunctionis CW 14 pars. 544ff

Jung, C. G. The Undiscovered Self, Mentor Books, Little Brown and Company Boston Mass. 1958

Jung, C. G. The Archetype and the Collective Unconscious Princeton University Press, 1981

Jung, C. G. Man and His Symbols, Doubleday, Garden City, NY 1964

Jung, C. G. The Portable Jung, Penguin Books, 1971

THE EGO AND THE BIBLE

Jung, C.G. The Structure of the Psyche, CW 8, par. 325

Luke, Helen. *The Inner Story,* Crossroads, New York 1982

Marks, Peter and Joanne. A centre for Conscious Care *Different Directions to Our Divinity,* http://www.centreconsciouscare.ca/index.html

McKenna, Megan. *Prophets, Words of Fire,* Orbis Books Maryknoll, NY 2001

Rohr, Richard. Daily Meditations, Splitting from Others, Tuesday February 25, 2014

"The Apocryphal New Testament" M.R. James-Translation and Notes Oxford: Clarendon Press, 1924 http://gnosis.org/library/inftoma.htm

The Gospel of Judas, Rodolphe Kasser, Marvin Meyer, Gregor Wurst, Bart D. Ehrman National Geographic Books, 2008

Jacobi, Jolanda. The Psychology of Jung, An Introduction, Yale University Press, 1943

Williams, Charles. *He Came Down From Heaven,* London: Faber and Faber 1950

Made in the USA
Lexington, KY
08 April 2015